LIVING WITH PURPOSE BIBLE STUDY

Isaiah

LIVING WITH PURPOSE BIBLE STUDY

Isaiah

Guideposts

Living with Purpose Bible Study: Isaiah

Published by Guideposts
100 Reserve Road, Suite E200
Danbury, CT 06810
Guideposts.org

Cover design by Judy Ross
Interior design by Judy Ross
Cover photo by CHIH CHIEH HSIAO/iStock
Typeset by Aptara, Inc.

ISBN 978-1-961442-90-0 (hardcover)
ISBN 978-1-961442-91-7 (softcover)
ISBN 978-1-961442-92-4 (ebook)

Printed and bound in the United States of America
$PrintCode

CONTENTS

About Living with Purpose Bible Study....2

An Overview of Isaiah....5

LESSON 1: ISAIAH 1:1–6:13
Isaiah: The Man and His Message.... 11

LESSON 2: ISAIAH 7:1–21:17; 23:1–18
Isaiah and the Nations.... 41

LESSON 3: ISAIAH 22:1–25; 24:1–32:20
Messages of Judgment and Hope.... 74

LESSON 4: ISAIAH 33:1–39:8
Israel and the Nations.... 107

LESSON 5: ISAIAH 40:1–45:25
Called to Comfort.... 137

LESSON 6: ISAIAH 46:1–53:12
The Servant of the Lord.... 172

LESSON 7: ISAIAH 54:1–59:21
The Ecstasy and the Agony of Freedom.... 210

LESSON 8: ISAIAH 60:1–66:24
Future Restoration of Zion.... 238

Acknowledgments.... 266

A Note from the Editors.... 267

About Living with Purpose Bible Study

For as long as humankind has existed, we have pondered our place in the universe. Poets and preachers, philosophers and scientists alike have explored the topic for generations. Our busy modern lives leave little time for contemplation, and yet we move through our lives with nagging questions in the back of our minds: *Why am I here? What am I meant to do with my life?*

Fyodor Dostoevsky wrote that the "mystery of human existence lies not in just staying alive, but in finding something to live for." You might wonder how living with purpose ties in with the Bible. That's because God's Word is a guidebook for life, and God Himself has a purpose—a unique mission—for and unique to you. Reading the Bible and seeking God through prayer are two of the main ways God speaks to people. And when we begin to seek God, when we pursue His truth, when we begin to live our lives in ways that reflect His love back to others, we begin to find that purpose. Finding our purpose is not a destination; it is a journey we'll travel until we leave this earth behind and go to our heavenly Father.

Most of us know something about the Bible. We might be able to quote verses that we memorized as kids. Many of us have read parts of it, have learned about it in Sunday school as both children and adults. But not as many of us *know* the Bible, and that is where this Bible study comes in.

"Bible study" is a term that can elicit a variety of responses. For some people, the feeling that comes is a daunting sense of intimidation, even fear, because we worry that the Bible will somehow find us wanting, less than, rejected. Maybe we've heard preachers wielding the Bible as a weapon, using it as a measuring rod and a dividing line that separates "us" from "them."

Guideposts' *Living with Purpose Bible Study* addresses these questions and concerns with a hope-filled, welcoming, inclusive voice, like the one you've grown to know and love from Guideposts' devotional books, story collections, magazines, and website.

Best of all, you'll discover that the writers of *Living with Purpose Bible Study* are experts not only in the depth of their Bible knowledge but also in sharing that knowledge in such a welcoming, winning way that you can't help but be drawn in.

The writers come alongside you as trusted friends, guiding you through each volume in that warm, inviting manner that only Guideposts could bring you.

Each volume in the study draws from five trusted translations of the Bible: the New International Version, New American Standard Bible, the Amplified Version, the English Standard Version, and the King James Version of the Bible. We encourage you to keep your favorite Bible translation on hand as you read each study chapter. The Bible passages you read act as the foundation from which the study writers' insights, information, and inspiration flow. You can read along with the writers as each chapter unfolds, or you can read all of the passages or verses included in the chapter prior to reading it. It's up to you; you can use the method that works best for you.

In addition, you'll find two distinct features to enhance your experience: "A Closer Look" entries bring context by presenting historical, geographical, or cultural information, and "Inspiration from Isaiah" entries demonstrate the spiritual insights people like you have gained from their knowledge of the biblical text. We've also provided lined writing spaces at the end of each lesson for you to jot down your own thoughts, questions, discoveries, and *aha* moments that happen as you read and study.

A final note: before you read each chapter, we encourage you to pray, asking that God will open your eyes and heart to what He has to say. Our prayer for you is that you find a new or renewed sense of purpose and grow closer to God as you deepen your understanding of God's Word by enjoying this *Living with Purpose Bible Study*.

—*The Editors of Guideposts*

An Overview of Isaiah

Isaiah is a big book—the sixth-longest Bible book in terms of word count and the longest book among the books of prophecy. Its length alone can make it seem a little daunting, and, like virtually all the prophetic writings in the Bible, it uses visual imagery to communicate its truths. And while we will see things that seem strange and quite different from the world we know, it is impossible to study this book and remain the same.

Isaiah is also an extremely important book, and was considered so by John the Baptist, Jesus, and the writers of our New Testament. In fact, scores of quotations from the book of Isaiah appear in the New Testament. Over the millennia since Isaiah's writing, it has been examined and studied by Bible scholars of many backgrounds and viewpoints.

There are rich rewards ahead for us as we study the book of Isaiah, and you will quickly see that you are probably more familiar with this book than you might think. It is chock-full of phrases that will sound familiar to many readers, in part because they have been quoted in numerous other sections of the Bible but also because they are the basis of numerous hymns that Christian people have sung for centuries, as well as modern worship songs. In addition, they make their way into our hearts and minds each Christmas in selections from Handel's stirring oratorio *Messiah.*

- "The grass withereth, the flower fadeth: but the word of our God shall stand forever."
- "They that wait upon the LORD shall renew their strength; they shall mount up with wings as eagles; they shall run, and not be weary; and they shall walk, and not faint."
- "Fear thou not; for I am with thee: be not dismayed; for I am thy God."
- "He was wounded for our transgressions, he was bruised for our iniquities: the chastisement of our peace was upon him; and with his stripes we are healed."
- "His name shall be called Wonderful, Counsellor, The mighty God, The everlasting Father, The Prince of Peace."

These and other well-known sentences from the book of Isaiah (quoted above in the familiar wording of the King James Version) have challenged and encouraged people of faith across the centuries, yet most of us have only a vague understanding of the central message of this amazing book.

Our purpose in these studies is to roll aside the curtain a bit and catch a glimpse of what the book of Isaiah meant to the people of ancient Israel and Judah from the eighth century BC forward and what its message means to us now.

Who Wrote the Book of Isaiah?

Throughout history, there have been differing schools of thought about the authorship of the book of Isaiah.

Going back hundreds, even thousands, of years, both Jewish and early Christian leaders accepted without question that the book of Isaiah was the work of one man, the prophet Isaiah, son of Amoz. Evidence in favor of this view includes the complete book of Isaiah, discovered among the Dead Sea Scrolls at Qumran in the mid-1940s. This ancient scroll, dating to around 175 BC, treated the book as one single, whole work, with no signs of the work itself being divided into sections.

In the eighteenth century, based on such factors as what they perceived to be different writing styles as well as contextual and historical clues, theologians first suggested the possibility of two different authors at two different times. German theologian Johann Christoph Döderlein proposed that chapters 1–39 were written by Isaiah, son of Amoz, while chapters 40–66 were the work of another, unknown prophet in the sixth century BC.

This prevailing view was largely displaced in the nineteenth and early twentieth centuries, when theologians such as Bernhard Duhm began proposing the idea that *three* distinct writers were responsible for the book, writing at three different times.

There was and still is broad, though not unanimous, agreement that the prophet Isaiah of Jerusalem is directly responsible for chapters 1–39 of the book that bears his name. Chapters 40–55, Duhm and others believed, was written by someone else, somewhat later, *during* the exile that took the Hebrew people to Babylon. They further suggested that chapters 56–66 were the writings of yet another author, *after* the Hebrews returned to their homeland.

In the last years of the twentieth century, this view began to lose favor and was supplanted again by the two-author theory. And in more recent years, the emphasis on the book's authorship has, at least to some degree, given way once more to viewing and studying the book, regardless of who wrote it, as a unified whole.

The book of Isaiah indeed forms a cohesive, unified whole with themes that include hope and salvation (indeed, Isaiah's name means "salvation of Yahweh" or "the Lord's salvation"); redemption and reconciliation; and God's steadfast love, comfort, and mercy.

A Dramatic Calling

Isaiah's prophetic ministry (chapters 1–39) occurred during one of the most momentous and turbulent periods of Jewish history. The northern kingdom of Israel had been conquered by the mighty Assyrian armies, which were also a threat to the southern kingdom of Judah. It was a time of immense political intrigue. Through it all Isaiah remained faithful to his calling.

Isaiah received his call from God "in the year that king Uzziah died"—somewhere around 742–740 BC—and his ministry continued until approximately 700 BC. It is thought that Isaiah may have been a relative of King Uzziah and was likely a member of Jerusalem's aristocracy. The Bible tells us that the prophet was married and had two sons.

Beginning with the prophet Isaiah's call to service, described in chapter 6, he came to an entirely new understanding of God's holiness. Until this time, the people of Israel and Judah understood God's holiness as His being separate or set apart from them. However, under Isaiah's prophetic teaching, God's holiness assumed moral implications.

In the Temple vision, when the young Isaiah heard the words "Holy, holy, holy, is the LORD of hosts: the whole earth is full of his glory," his immediate reaction was "Woe is me! for I am undone; because I am a man of unclean lips, and I dwell in the midst of a people of unclean lips" (6:3, 5, KJV). From then on, Isaiah's frequent designation for God was "the Holy One of Israel." He used this title twelve times in the first thirty-nine chapters of the book, and it appears thirteen times in the remainder of the book.

It was this acute awareness of God's holiness that made the prophet so conscious of the sin of the people of Judah. They had turned their backs on the Holy One and had refused to hear His word or behave in obedience to His will.

The prophet knew there was just one answer to their rebellion, and that was to turn to the Lord God, who was "the God of your salvation" (Isaiah 17:10, ESV). And salvation is a significant theme in the entire Isaiah drama. Even as Isaiah thundered against everything that violated God's holiness and saw the inevitability of God's judgment, he was, at the same time, a prophet of hope because of his understanding of the Holy One as Redeemer and Savior.

As Christians, we see in Isaiah's prophetic hope the coming Messiah. Though Isaiah likely expected the Messiah to come in his lifetime, we know his hope was actually fulfilled in Bethlehem seven centuries later.

The Faithful Few

The setting for chapters 40–55 seems to be toward the end of the Babylonian captivity. Here we have some of the most magnificent poetry in all of the Old Testament as Isaiah passionately extols God as the Creator of the universe and the One in charge of all history. It is little wonder that Handel leaned so heavily on Isaiah's words in the *Messiah* oratorio.

The final section of the book of Isaiah, chapters 56–66, sees the Hebrews returned from exile and at home in Jerusalem and Judah. Here we gain insight into the thinking and actions of the people as they forged a new life in their homeland with great emphasis on the importance of worship and righteous living. And it is here we catch a model of our witness as the prophet so beautifully pictures his mission then: "The Spirit of the Sovereign LORD is on me, because the LORD has anointed me to proclaim good news to the poor. He has sent me to bind up the brokenhearted, to proclaim freedom for the captives and release from darkness for the prisoners, to proclaim the year of the LORD's favor and the day of vengeance of our God, to comfort all who mourn" (61:1–2, NIV).

Threaded throughout the book of Isaiah and especially in the prophetic word that informs chapters 1–39 is the fact that in the face of all that would happen there, some people would remain faithful to God—the remnant that would "lean on the LORD, the Holy One of Israel, in truth . . . the remnant of Jacob" that would return "to the mighty God" (10:20–21, ESV).

These were the faithful few who remained true to God under all sorts of circumstances. To be a part of that faithful few—"a remnant, chosen by grace" (Romans 11:5, ESV)—is still the mission of God's people today.

We invite you now to collect your favorite Bible or Bibles, pour yourself a cup of tea or coffee, and find a comfortable, quiet place to sit as we begin our study of Isaiah together.

LESSON 1: ISAIAH 1:1–6:13

Isaiah: The Man and His Message

Father, help me to be attuned and faithful to Your calling for my life. Amen.

Isaiah occupies a significant place in God's Word. In our Bible it stands as the first of the collection of prophetic books, followed by Jeremiah, Ezekiel, Daniel, and the twelve so-called Minor Prophets. Its position as the first of the prophetic books is testimony to the high esteem it has enjoyed across the centuries.

The sixty-six chapters of the book of Isaiah cover a period of slightly more than two centuries—from the time of the prophet's call in 742 BC (6:1) to beyond Cyrus's conquest of Babylon and the liberation of the Jewish exiles in 539 BC (45:1–6). Few books of the Bible cover such an extended period of time. To properly understand the message of Isaiah, it will be helpful to have a brief overview of the times and culture of eighth-century BC Israel and Judah.

Isaiah in His Historical Setting

The few facts that we know about Isaiah's life and ministry are found in Isaiah 1:1; 6:1–8:22; 20:1–6; 36:1–39:8; and 2 Kings

19:1–20:21. The writings in Isaiah 36:1–39:8 and in 2 Kings 19:1–20:21 are parallel accounts of the same events and are to be dated near the end of Isaiah's ministry.

The Length of Isaiah's Ministry

At the very beginning of our study we learn that Isaiah prophesied during the reigns of Uzziah (783–742 BC), Jotham (742–735 BC), Ahaz (735–715 BC), and Hezekiah (715–687 BC) (1:1). Isaiah's inaugural vision (6:1–13) is dated "in the year that King Uzziah died" (742 BC).

Assuming that he was perhaps around 30 years old at the time of his call to the Lord's service, his birth would have occurred around 770 BC, during Uzziah's reign as king of Judah. The last dated events in his ministry occurred in 701 BC, the year King Sennacherib of Assyria invaded Judah and laid siege to Jerusalem (Isaiah 36:1–39:8). This means that Isaiah was active over a period of at least forty years. Few prophets had such a long ministry or lived to such a ripe old age.

The Circumstances of Isaiah's Death

There is a rabbinic tradition that Isaiah was put to death by Manasseh, the evil son and successor of King Hezekiah (see 2 Kings 21:1–16). This story is recorded in a second-century AD Jewish work known as "The Martyrdom of Isaiah." It reports that the aged prophet was sawed apart by Manasseh's men after he had hidden himself in a hollow tree. There is perhaps a reference to this story in Hebrews 11:37.

Isaiah's Family

The opening verse of the book tells us that Isaiah's father was named Amoz (not to be confused with the prophet Amos). An ancient Jewish tradition states that Isaiah's father was a brother to Amaziah, the father of Azariah, another name for Uzziah (see 2 Kings 14:17–22). If this is true, it means that Isaiah was of royal descent and was related to the kings of Judah. However, there is no biblical evidence to support the claim. While Isaiah had ready access to the courts of kings, so did many other Old Testament prophets (see 2 Samuel 12:1–15; Jeremiah 38:14–28).

Isaiah was married, and his wife was referred to as "the prophetess" (8:3). Two suggestions have been made as to why she was called a prophetess. The first is that like Miriam (see Exodus 15:20–21) and Huldah (see 2 Kings 22:14–20), she may actually have fulfilled a prophetic role of her own. Certain women served as prophetesses even in New Testament times (see Acts 21:8–9). The other suggestion is that Isaiah's wife may have been called a prophetess simply because she was married to a prophet. We have no way of knowing which of these ideas is correct.

Isaiah and his wife had two sons. Like the children of Hosea (see Hosea 1:2–9), Isaiah's sons were given symbolic names. The first was named Shear-jashub (7:3), meaning "a remnant shall return." It may have meant that either a remnant among the people would repent and return to the Lord or that a remnant would return from exile. The other son was named Maher-shalal-hash-baz (8:1–4), which may be translated, "The spoil speeds, the prey hastes." His name was a message of judgment against Damascus (Syria) and Samaria (the northern kingdom of Israel) in the crisis that occurred in 735–734 BC. It spoke of the downfall of these two enemies of the southern kingdom of Judah. The names of Isaiah's two sons conveyed messages of hope to the hard-pressed citizens of Jerusalem and Judah and were reminders of God's love and concern for them.

The Assyrian Threat

Isaiah lived out his entire career during the period of Assyrian domination of the Middle East. The great Assyrian Empire was ruled by Tiglath-Pileser III from 745 to 727 BC. Tiglath-Pileser was fierce, cruel, and diabolically clever in his efforts to impose his will on the smaller nations around him. The military campaigns that he and his successors waged kept Palestine and surrounding areas in a state of constant turmoil throughout most of Isaiah's lifetime.

Isaiah's First Period of Crisis

The prophet experienced four periods of crisis that were especially severe. The first came in the years between 735 and 732 BC. Around 735 BC, Pekah, king of Israel, and Rezin, king of Syria, decided to form an alliance against the Assyrians. They tried to force Ahaz, king of Judah, to join them. When he refused, they launched an attack against Jerusalem in an effort to unseat him (Isaiah 7:1; 2 Kings 16:5).

King Ahaz was young and inexperienced, and the presence of invading armies on his soil filled him with panic (Isaiah 7:2).

As he went out to inspect Jerusalem's water system in preparation for the expected attack upon the city, he was met by Isaiah and his son Shear-jashub (Isaiah 7:3). Isaiah tried but failed to win over the king to a bold policy of trust in the Lord. His message was simple, apparently too simple for Ahaz: trust in the Lord; be quiet and keep calm (Isaiah 7:4–9). Disregarding the prophet's advice, Ahaz appealed directly to Tiglath-Pileser for help against Pekah and Rezin (2 Kings 16:7). His appeal was reinforced by a generous gift of silver and gold (2 Kings 16:8). The Assyrian king was only too glad to oblige, and around 732 BC he conquered Damascus, exiled the people, and killed the king (2 Kings 16:9). By this time Pekah had been assassinated, and Hoshea had taken his place as king of Israel (2 Kings 15:29–31). Tiglath-Pileser recognized Hoshea as the new Israelite king and made him his vassal. The northern kingdom of Israel had now been incorporated into the vast Assyrian Empire, and it never again regained its independence.

King Ahaz's appeal for help from Tiglath-Pileser enabled him to remain on the throne in Jerusalem, but only at the cost of heavy taxation and permanent subjection to the Assyrians (2 Kings 16:10–18). His failure to follow Isaiah's advice proved to be a costly blunder both for him and for the southern kingdom of Judah.

Isaiah's Second Period of Crisis

The second crisis that occurred during Isaiah's career was the fall of the northern kingdom of Israel to the Assyrians in 722 BC. Although Judah was not directly involved, the final collapse of Israel placed the Assyrians at her northern frontier, where they continued to threaten her existence for the next century or so. The downfall of Israel constituted a crisis that Isaiah could not afford to overlook as he ministered to the people of Judah.

The immediate cause of Israel's downfall was King Hoshea's revolt against Shalmaneser V, the son and successor of Tiglath-Pileser and the ruler of the Assyrian Empire from 727 to 722 BC. Hoshea revolted against Assyria around 726 BC, apparently expecting to receive support from the Egyptians (Isaiah 30:1–31:9; 2 Kings 17:4).

Shalmaneser and his Assyrian army attacked Israel around 725 BC, and after a three-year siege to Samaria, the city was conquered and Hoshea was taken prisoner. Isaiah had tried to warn the people of Israel of their peril, but they ignored his warning and were defeated (Isaiah 9:8–10:4; 17:1–11; 28:1–4; 2 Kings 17:5–6).

During the siege of Samaria, Sargon II (722–705 BC) succeeded Shalmaneser as king over the Assyrian Empire.

Isaiah's Third Period of Crisis

The third crisis during Isaiah's ministry came in 711 BC. Four years earlier, in 715 BC, while Sargon was engaged in battle elsewhere, rebellion against Assyria was again fomented in southern Palestine. It was centered in the city-state of Ashdod, whose king had apparently received offers of help from Egypt and Ethiopia.

King Ahaz of Judah had by now been replaced by Hezekiah (715–687 BC). The king of Ashdod sought the support of

Judah and other neighboring states against Assyria. Isaiah advised Hezekiah against giving such support, believing that in the end it would be disastrous for Judah (Isaiah 20:1–6).

By 711 BC, Sargon moved to crush this rebellion. When his troops reached Ashdod, its king took refuge in Egypt, only to be captured and handed over to the Assyrians. Sargon celebrated his victory at Ashdod and the crushing of the rebellion by erecting a black basalt pillar inscribed with a glowing account of his victory. (Archaeologists discovered pieces of this pillar at the ancient site of Ashdod in 1963.) We don't know how deeply Hezekiah became involved in the Ashdod rebellion, but apparently Judah suffered some reprisals from the Assyrians (Isaiah 22:1–14).

Isaiah's Fourth Period of Crisis

The fourth and most serious crisis during Isaiah's prophetic ministry came in 701 BC. The ruling king of the Assyrian Empire at that time was Sennacherib (705–681 BC). When he succeeded Sargon, Sennacherib was faced with widespread rebellion throughout the Assyrian Empire. This included a full-scale revolt by Hezekiah, king of Judah. This time Hezekiah seems to have had the support of Isaiah in his rebellion against Assyria.

Sennacherib moved in 701 BC to quell the rebellion. One of his armies marched down the Philistine coast and defeated the Egyptians. A second army moved across Samaria and approached Jerusalem from the north (Isaiah 10:28–34). In the course of the campaign, Sennacherib claimed to have destroyed forty-six cities of Judah. And in writing about his siege at Jerusalem, Sennacherib declared, "Hezekiah I made a prisoner in Jerusalem, his royal residence, like a bird in a cage." The Isaiah writer probably referred to the devastation of the land at this time, as he spoke of Jerusalem being left "like a booth in a vineyard, like a lodge in a cucumber field, like a besieged city" (1:8, ESV).

The prophet Isaiah's role in these events is described in chapters 36:1–37:38 of the book of Isaiah and in the parallel passages in 2 Kings 18:13–19:37. The prophet was vindicated in his encouragement of Hezekiah when a plague of death struck the Assyrian army and caused it to withdraw from the siege at Jerusalem as suddenly as it had come (Isaiah 37:33–37; 2 Kings 19:32–36). We don't know that Isaiah engaged in any other prophetic activity after these events. The remainder of the book of Isaiah (chapters 40–66) describes events that took place over a century and a half after Isaiah's death.

In summarizing the chronological arrangement of the book of Isaiah, we may say that generally speaking, chapters 1–6 come from the reign of Uzziah (783–742 BC), chapters 7–14 are in the period of Ahaz (735–715 BC), chapters 15–33 and 36–39 refer to events during the reign of King Hezekiah (715–687 BC), and chapters 34–35 and 40–66 cover the period of Cyrus and beyond (550–520 BC).

The Threat from Within

In addition to the external threat from the Assyrians, Isaiah's listeners were faced with an even greater threat from within: moral collapse and spiritual decay.

The people to whom Isaiah preached were laboring under four false assumptions:

1. They thought that the covenant given to Moses on Mount Sinai bound God to the people of Israel with ties that could not be broken.
2. They thought they were fully discharging their covenant obligations by coming to the Temple from time to time to make the appropriate sacrifices.
3. They believed "the day of the Lord" was near at hand and that it would be a time of triumph for Israel and for God.
4. They thought that no matter how difficult the situation became, God would never allow Jerusalem to be captured or destroyed. There was, so they believed, a kind of magic circle around the city that guaranteed its future.

It was against the background of these false hopes and assumptions that Isaiah's ministry unfolded.

The Central Teachings of Isaiah

The prophets were not systematic theologians, and we must not try to cast them in that role. At the same time, it is helpful in our study to look at the central truths in Isaiah's preaching.

(1) *The Holiness of the Lord.* More than any other prophet, Isaiah stressed the absolute holiness of God. To be holy means to be different, distinct, and set apart. To say that the Lord is holy means first of all that He is God and not human. The writer of the book of Hosea put it this way, "I am God and not a man, the Holy One in your midst, and I will not come in wrath" (11:9, ESV). God is set apart from all created things and rules over them.

We read that Isaiah was filled with an overpowering sense of the Lord's holiness at the time of his call to service (see 6:3). He characteristically referred to the Lord as "the Holy One of Israel," a title used some thirty times throughout the book (see 1:4; 10:20; 12:6; 17:7; 31:1).

(2) *The Lord as Ruler of History.* Isaiah believed that the Holy One of Israel was firmly in charge of the affairs of people and of nations. He saw God directing all the movements of history in accordance with His purpose to establish His rule on earth. It was true that at times it seemed that certain pagan nations appeared to prevail, but it was also clear that God remained in charge. The mighty Assyrians, though they were at the zenith of their power, were but "the rod" and "the club" (NIV) that God used to chastise His people (see 10:5–11). Then when God had finished correcting His people, He would break "the rod" and cast it aside (see 10:12–19).

God's ultimate purpose was that the people in all the nations, including Israel, would acknowledge Him as the supreme Lord of history and worship Him (see 2:2–4; 18:7; 19:19–25).

(3) *The Folly of Human Pride.* Isaiah made it clear that the ultimate sin is pride—pride in one's own power, pride in one's own wisdom, and pride in one's own achievements. He spoke of the coming day of the Lord as a time when human pride would be judged and "lofty pride" of humanity would "be brought low" (2:12–17, ESV). In other words, Assyria, drunk with its own power and might, would be humbled (see 10:12–19). The pride of the nation of Moab, Israel's enemy on the eastern border, would also be humbled (see 16:6–7).

And mighty Babylon, who boasted, "'I am, and there is none besides me" (47:8, NIV), would be brought down from its lofty perch and made "to sit on the ground" (47:1, NIV). It was the Lord's purpose to crush all monuments to human pride and to stand alone as the Exalted and Holy One of Israel.

As a corollary to the Lord's hatred of human pride, Isaiah taught that He was always available to the meek and lowly of the earth. Near the end of the book, the writer worded it this way: "For thus says the One who is high and lifted up, who inhabits eternity, whose name is Holy: 'I dwell in the high and holy place, and also with him who is of a contrite and lowly spirit, to revive the spirit of the lowly, and to revive the heart of the contrite'" (57:15, ESV).

(4) *The True Service of God.* One of Isaiah's basic teachings was that true service to God consisted of service to humankind. This applied especially to acts of justice and mercy performed on behalf of the poor and oppressed, the homeless, the widows, and orphans. These were the defenseless members of society for whom the system offered little protection and little support.

On the other hand, Isaiah's contemporaries believed that the true service of God consisted of acts of worship performed at a central sanctuary with a duly ordained priesthood offering the prescribed sacrifices. They also believed they were fully accepted by God because they participated in such services of worship. To them, right rituals were of far greater importance than right living.

But Isaiah had an entirely different view of what it meant to be rightly related to God. To him true worship included far more than offering sacrifices and keeping holy days (see 1:11, 14). Rather, a person who would be truly pleasing to God must "learn to do good; seek justice, correct oppression; bring justice to the fatherless, plead the widow's cause" (1:17, ESV). What God wanted most from His people was "judgment" or justice and "righteousness" (see 5:7). Without these, all acts of worship were but empty mockery.

(5) *The Centrality of Faith.* Perhaps more than any other Hebrew prophet, Isaiah presented faith as the believer's only adequate response to God. In crisis after crisis, Isaiah proclaimed faith in God as the only alternative to frustration and defeat. This was the heart of his advice to King Ahaz in 735 BC (see 7:9) and to King Hezekiah in 701 BC (see 28:16; 30:15). Isaiah believed that the feverish efforts of these kings to strengthen the defenses of Jerusalem, along with their endless appeals to foreign powers for help, indicated an attitude of unbelief. They were guilty of placing the power of humans above the power of God. Faith in God with humble obedience to His will was Israel's only road to social and political stability.

(6) *The Coming Messiah.* More than any other prophet, Isaiah was responsible for the development of the messianic hope in the Old Testament. He was one of the first, if not the first, of the prophets to link the coming of the Messiah and the dream of an ideal age of righteousness and peace.

The messianic hope of the Old Testament, to which Isaiah contributed so much, consisted of the belief that in days to come God would raise up a righteous king from the line of David to rule over His people. Righteousness and peace would characterize the rule of this messianic king, and his dominion would extend throughout the earth. This hope tended to shine brightest when the Israelites' circumstances were the darkest. Perhaps this helps to explain why it was so strong against the background of the Assyrian threat of the eighth century BC.

Isaiah's messianic expectation was born largely of his disappointment in the kings who ruled Judah during his lifetime. In a famous trilogy of messianic passages, he speaks of the Messiah's birth (7:10–16), of His accession to the throne (9:2–7), and of His righteous rule (11:1–9). Be sure to take a moment now and reread these familiar verses.

We get the impression from a close study of these verses that Isaiah expected those events to take place during his lifetime. Most certainly he had no way of knowing that their fulfillment would occur seven centuries later when in the fullness of time the Messiah did come and the glories of His kingdom far outshone even the fondest expectations of the prophet.

Now, as we move on to look more closely into the writings of Isaiah, we will do something rather unusual: we will skip forward and begin our study with chapter 6, which introduces Isaiah's call and commission. Then, after we have examined that important event in Isaiah's life, we will move back to the beginning and focus on the prophet's early preaching.

Isaiah's Call and Commission (6:1–13)

In all the literature of the Old Testament there is nothing quite like the account of Isaiah's call and commission as found in this part of our scripture lesson. Here the Law, the prophets, and the psalms all converge. We are reminded of the Law by the vision of the Temple, the altar, and the burning coals. The prophetic literature contains no words more inspiring than this classic account of a prophet's call. And the psalms are made up largely of two basic elements—praise and petition—and both are present here.

Isaiah's Vision of God

Isaiah's vision is dated in the year that King Uzziah died (6:1). Uzziah had been a good king and had reigned approximately forty years in Jerusalem (783–742 BC). A summary account of his extraordinary accomplishments is given in 2 Kings 15:1–7 and 2 Chronicles 26. It is likely Isaiah was born around the middle of Uzziah's reign.

Since the concept of an absolute monarchy is alien to most people in our modern culture, it is hard for us to understand the significance of the king in ancient society. He was a father figure to his subjects. From him, blessing and strength went out to the whole nation. For this reason, the death of a good king like Uzziah must have caused intense shock and grief for the people of Judah. Perhaps the reaction could be compared to that of many people when they heard the news of the assassination of President John F. Kennedy in 1963, the *Challenger* shuttle disaster in 1986, or the destruction of the World Trade Center towers in 2001.

Moved by the death of the great king, Isaiah made his way into the Temple and there received a vision that transformed his life. While grieving over a dead king and an empty throne, he caught a vision of a heavenly throne and of a divine King who never dies. Judah's human kings might come and go in an endless procession, but this King would reign forever.

In colorful language that is rich in metaphor, Isaiah tells us that around the heavenly throne there were choirs of seraphim, a word descriptive of some form of fiery creatures. Each one had three pairs of wings, which symbolized reverence, modesty, and service. The seraphim sang in antiphony as they echoed the praise of God's holiness (6:2–4).

Isaiah's Vision of Himself

According to the prophet's next words, his vision of God's holiness was accompanied by an overwhelming vision of himself (6:5–7). In stark contrast to the divine and awesome holiness of God, he caught a vision of his own unholiness. And that vision was more than he could stand as he cried out in distress, "Woe to me, for I am ruined!" (6:5, NASB). The word translated "ruined" in our text means to be cut off, cut down, destroyed, or doomed. Isaiah felt that for a person as sinful as he to look at a majestic and holy God meant sure death.

But Isaiah had failed to make allowance for God's mercy. Here we understand that God heard his cry, cleansed his lips, and forgave his sin. The way this was done is significant. We're told that one of the seraphim flew to the Temple altar, picked up a burning coal, pressed it against Isaiah's lips, and said, "Behold, this has touched your lips; and your guilt is taken away and atonement is made for your sin" (6:7, NASB). There was no painless way to remove Isaiah's guilt, even as there is no painless way to remove our guilt. Forgiveness must often be secured at the price of suffering and even death, otherwise the Son of Man would not have had to endure the Cross.

Isaiah's Vision of a World in Need

The center and climax of Isaiah's vision and call to service comes in verse 8, "I heard the voice of the Lord, saying, Whom shall I send, and who will go for us? Then said I, Here am I; send me" (6:8, KJV). Instead of pleading his inadequacy as Moses and Jeremiah had done, Isaiah volunteered to be sent even before he understood what this might involve. God had taken care of his past; he was now willing to let Him have his future.

Gratitude has always been the most effective motivation for service. When we are forgiven much, we love much. We love Him because He first loved us (see 1 John 4:19). Our willingness to serve can always be measured by our gratitude for divine forgiveness.

It was only after Isaiah had committed himself to be God's messenger to his people that he learned what his message was to be. First, he was to make it clear that they were to be judged by a holy God for their sins and it was too late to repent (6:9–10). Then he followed the prediction of the devastation of their land (6:11–13). Most certainly, Isaiah was given a profound message for his audience.

Isaiah's Early Preaching (1:1–5:30)

While it is not possible to give a specific date to all that occurs in this part of our scripture lesson, at least some of what is said belongs to Isaiah's early ministry. It is readily apparent that most of his early messages were steeped in gloom and doom.

God's Case against His People

The book of Isaiah opens with a description of the rebellion of the people of Judah and its dire consequences. And we first read that their sin was rooted in ingratitude. In vivid language the prophet says they didn't even have as much gratitude as an ox or an ass for the food that was in their crib. The indictment against them is awesome: "Woe to the sinful nation, a people whose guilt is great, a brood of evildoers, children given to corruption! They have forsaken the LORD; they have spurned the Holy One of Israel and turned their backs on him" (1:4, NIV).

Next, the consequences of their sin are described (1:5–9). The people of Judah were like a rebellious child whose father had disciplined it until its body was covered with bruises and wounds. But still the child continued to rebel, apparently bent on self-destruction. Our picture here is one of pain and desolation and may well be associated with the invasion of Sennacherib in 701 BC.

A Fearsome Word

We shift now to a new setting (1:10–20). The courts of the Temple echoed with the prayers of the people as they went about their ritual duty in the offering of sacrifices. Just when they thought their actions were most pleasing to God, Isaiah lambasted them and accused them of being "rulers of Sodom" and "people of Gomorrah" (1:10, NIV)—Sodom and Gomorrah symbolizing glaring and vulgar immorality.

Then the prophet went on to denounce their sacrifices (1:11), their solemn assemblies (1:13–14), and even their prayers (1:15) as being an offense to God because these were divorced from righteous living. If they would be truly pleasing to God, he told them, let them cleanse themselves, abandon their evil ways, learn to do good, and champion the cause of the poor and oppressed in society (1:16–17). The eighth-century prophets placed far more importance on feeding the poor, looking after orphans and widows, and giving attention to the oppressed than they did on keeping the laws and worshipping a certain way.

The prophet still offers repentance as an alternative to destruction (1:18–20). And unless they repent, the people will reap the bitter fruits of their actions. Verse 31 makes it clear that sin always brings its own destruction. Sinners, here referred to as "the strong" (ESV) or "the mighty" (NIV), "become like flax fiber" (NASB) or tinder. Their evil deeds provide the spark that ignites them. And once the fires of judgment have been kindled, no human effort can put them out.

A Vision of World Peace

Next, Isaiah gives us a marvelous vision of world peace (2:1–5). This same prophecy, in a slightly expanded form, occurs in Micah 4:1–7. Since Isaiah and Micah were contemporaries, it is impossible to know which of them may have first spoken these words. It may even be possible that both borrowed them from an anonymous source.

Four conclusions can be drawn from this great poem about peace:

1. Peace is possible only in a world in which the sovereignty of God is acknowledged.
2. Peace rests not upon human programs alone but upon obedience to the revelation of God's will and purpose.
3. To be effective, peace must be accompanied by a reduction of arms on the part of all nations.
4. When the dream of peace is fulfilled, there will be freedom from hunger and from fear (see Micah 4:4). The most effective war on poverty would be an all-out war on war itself.

This is God's dream for the world. May it also be ours?

The Day of the Lord

The term "the day of the Lord" occurs frequently in the Old Testament, especially in the prophets. Sometimes it is found in abbreviated form as "the day," or "that day" (see Isaiah 2:11, 12, 17, 20). Traditionally, it refers to those times when God intervenes in human history to judge the wicked and to liberate the oppressed. Generally speaking, the element of judgment is more prominent than that of deliverance in the references to this "day" (see Amos 5:18–20; Zephaniah 1:14–15). Quite likely all of us can think of recent events in world history that might be classified as "days of the Lord"—times when nations and people were judged because of their sinfulness and stupidity.

The "day of the Lord" was necessary in Isaiah's time because the people of Israel and Judah had become rich, idolatrous, and proud (2:6–9). The prophet announced that all things high and mighty on this earth were moving steadily toward the day when they would be destroyed (2:10–21). When the dust of their destruction had settled, "the LORD alone will be exalted" (2:11, 17, NASB).

It is important to remember that human achievements, even the noblest and most complex, are only temporal—they are here today and gone tomorrow—but so often we make the mistake of thinking of them as eternal. In our lust for power and in the headiness over achievements in constructing vast bridges and skyscrapers, space travel and planetary probes, instant communication across the globe, and immediate access to immense stores of knowledge at the tap of a finger, our value systems can so easily go on tilt because we forget that in this world of change and decay, God alone is eternal. The work of our hands—our achievements—may soon disappear, but the greatness of God lasts forever.

Anarchy and the Collapse of Society

The prophet now focuses his attention and warning on what he sees as the collapse of Judean society (3:1–4:1). Another caption for this section could well be "The Crisis of Leadership." It was a time when competent leadership had disappeared and the government of Judah fell into the hands of incompetent weaklings. It has been suggested that such a condition existed at the beginning of the reign of Ahaz (735–715 BC), who was only 20 years of age when he came to power (2 Kings 16:2).

Contributing to this state of anarchy in Judah was the removal of four groups of leaders who would normally function as the pillars of society. These were the military leaders, the elders, the counselors, and the prophets (3:1–3). In their place, according to Isaiah, were "children" and "babes" (3:4, KJV)—people too immature and unprepared to be leaders. Consequently, there was political and social confusion (3:5–15). An old adage declares, "The people always get the kinds of leaders they deserve." Assuming there's a measure of truth to that, what does this say about us when it comes to some of the political and religious leaders in our world today?

The Doyennes of Jerusalem

Contributing to the political and social crisis in Jerusalem were the wealthy, influential "daughters of Zion" (ESV), the upper-crust women who lived in the exclusive part of the city near the Temple area. These were the aristocratic socialites whom Isaiah was condemning for their immodest behavior (3:16–4:1). Isaiah was bold enough to speak out against the vulgar excesses of these women who were disrupting Jerusalem society.

Jerusalem Restored

Once again, the prophet turns his attention to the future—that "day of the Lord"—when Jerusalem will be restored to its former beauty and glory (4:2–6). Once more, in the midst of confusion and gloom, the prophet sounds a high note of hope. He writes, "Then the LORD will create over all of Mount Zion and over those who assemble there a cloud of smoke by day and a glow of flaming fire by night; over everything the glory will be a canopy" (4:5, NIV). These words are reminiscent of the presence of God with the people of Israel after the Exodus and during their time in the wilderness. The cloud, smoke, flaming fire, and glory are all symbolic of the presence of God. And as the Apostle Paul said to the Christians in Rome, "If God be for us, who can be against us?" (Romans 8:31, KJV).

The Song of the Vineyard

It is possible that Isaiah actually sang this song to the crowds gathered in Jerusalem at the time of the autumn festival known as the Feast of Tabernacles (5:1–7). It would have been a most effective way to capture the attention of farmers bringing the firstfruits of their harvest to the Lord. They understood what the prophet meant as he sang of the care with which a farmer had tended his vineyard. However, by listening to him they fell into the trap that he had carefully laid for them.

Isaiah sang about a farmer who had scrupulously followed all these steps. He had chosen a fertile field, prepared the soil and removed the stones, planted the choicest variety of vines, built a watchtower in the midst of it, and hewn out a wine vat for the harvesting of the crop (5:1–2). All his efforts were wasted, however, for when harvesttime came he discovered that the grapes were putrid-tasting and the wine was worthless.

Having described a situation that the farmers in his audience could understand and appreciate, Isaiah asked them to rule on whether he would be justified in just abandoning the vineyard (5:5–6). By removing the protective walls and by no longer pruning or cultivating the vines, it would revert to a natural but unproductive state. There is no more effective way to destroy a vineyard or an orchard than to abandon it and leave it to its own fate.

The prophet was saying that this was the way God intended to judge the people of Judah. He would simply withdraw His protection and care from them. They would be abandoned to manage their affairs without Him. The Lord had expected the Israelites to produce a harvest of justice and righteousness, but instead they had produced a bitter harvest of oppression leading to despair.

Grapes of Wrath

Having driven his point home, in a series of six "woes," Isaiah gave a more detailed account of Judah's sin (5:8–25).

First, woe to the greedy land-grabbers (5:8–10)! The prophet condemned those who acquired house after house and field after field so as to enjoy the privacy of their splendid estates. Without specifically saying so, he implied that this was done through dishonest means (see Micah 2:1–2, 8–9).

Their greed, however, would be self-defeating (5:9–10). Their mansions would soon stand empty and their fields would lose their productivity. These verses are a classic example of a futility curse, where an action undertaken for a desired effect produces results directly opposed to it. It is a most effective way to describe the futility of a life of sin and oppression.

Second, woe to those who chase after strong drink (5:11–17)! This woe was directed at Judah's heavy drinkers. Their parties were nothing but occasions for getting drunk to the sound of music. Their drinking began early in the day and continued late into the night until their minds were inflamed with wine. As a result of their drunkenness, they were unaware that God was still working in their midst. "They do not pay attention to the deeds of the Lord, nor do they consider the work of His hands" (5:12, NASB). They were oblivious to the divine judgment that was about to strike them.

Third, woe to those who work at sin and make a mockery of God (5:18–19)! Sinners were described as dragging their sin behind them as if they were harnessed to it with cart ropes. At the same time, they defiantly challenged God to do anything about it. Their defiance was the equivalent to thumbing one's nose in the face of God.

Fourth, woe to the morally color-blind (5:20)! This was addressed to those who were no longer capable of making moral distinctions. How forcefully it speaks to the modern world with its moral relativity and its situational ethics. How tragic it is for a person to no longer be able to distinguish between good and evil, between light and darkness, between bitter and sweet. Such a person is doomed to a life that is confused, obscure, and insipid.

Fifth, woe to "those who are wise in their own eyes" (5:21, ESV)! These were Israel's self-made successes. They considered themselves to be wise but were actually stupid, never coming to a knowledge of the truth.

Sixth, woe to those who are expert at mixing wine and also at perverting justice (5:22–25)! These were Israel's people of distinction, her connoisseurs of good wine. But while they knew how to choose their wine, they also knew how to pervert justice. A gift to the judge, a secret bribe—and they always won their cases in court. However, the Holy One of Israel, their heavenly Judge, was not as easily swayed as the earthly judge (see 5:24). In fact, He had already passed sentence on them, and their day of judgment would be a day of unspeakable agony and horror (5:25). They, along with the rest of the nation, would be judged by their actions—by the fruits they had produced.

The Lesson for Today

While the words and prophecies of Isaiah we have been studying in this lesson were most likely written around twenty-seven hundred years ago to a people and culture far different from ours, there is a strange and almost eerie up-to-date sound in what we have read. There are great similarities in what was happening in Israel and Judah to the mindsets and attitudes and actions that prevail in so much of our twenty-first-century world.

Isaiah was sorely distressed over a religion that failed to move beyond form and ritual to an authentic concern for justice and honesty in the nitty-gritty affairs of daily living. He spoke out rigorously against their disregard for the poor and underprivileged. And as we reflect on this part of his message, we see unflattering parallels to religious and social patterns in society today. We cannot fulfill the responsibilities of our faith or live out our love for the Lord and fail to act on behalf of the world's hungry and needy.

In this the prophet was very much in tune with the words of Jesus when in His parable He rejected those who had failed to respond to people's needs. These piercing words of His have echoed across the centuries: "For I was hungry and you gave me nothing to eat, I was thirsty and you gave me nothing to drink, I was a stranger and you did not invite me in, I needed clothes and you did not clothe me, I was sick and in prison and you did not look after me" (Matthew 25:42–43, NIV).

At that point Jesus anticipated His listeners' questions as He went on to say, "They also will answer, 'Lord, when did we see you hungry or thirsty or a stranger or needing clothes or sick or in prison, and did not help you?'"

Note His response to their questions: "Truly I tell you, whatever you did not do for one of the least of these, you did not do for me" (Matthew 25:44–45, NIV).

To reflect on Isaiah's message in this first lesson and our Lord's words in the parable is to be reminded of our responsibilities as Christians today. Projected on our television screens and cell phone displays are the faces of starving people in impoverished, famine-stricken, or war-torn countries; the hungry and unhoused in our own towns and cities; and those who, for any number of reasons in our challenging society, can't make ends meet. These are scenes that make us uncomfortable and uneasy, but they are scenes we dare not ignore. The prophet's call to us is that "our walk must act out our talk."

Lord, let my outward actions reflect my inward convictions, my commitment to You, and my regard for Your Word. AMEN.

INSPIRATION FROM ISAIAH

And there will be a tabernacle for shade in the daytime from the heat, for a place of refuge, and for a shelter from storm and rain.

—Isaiah 4:6 (NKJV)

The Red Abbey is named for its red sandstone. It is one of the oldest surviving structures in Cork City, Ireland, and dates back to the thirteenth century. As amazing as those facts were when I saw the abbey during my first trip to Ireland, something else comes to mind whenever I think of that landmark. I remember the coo of a pigeon coming from an archway, hearing someone say, "I see a bird up there," snapping a photo not knowing what would show up in it, and zooming in to discover I'd captured a perfectly clear picture of a pigeon peeking out of a hole in the sandstone.

The centuries-old structure was destroyed by a fire in the late 1700s (by then it was a sugar refinery), and the three hundred pieces of lead shot found during an excavation indicate that it endured many battles. With this history, it fascinated me to know that the Red Abbey was providing a nesting place for that pigeon and possibly even her babies. Sure, the pigeons most likely came to the abbey knowing Cork is a bustling city full of locals and tourists who would throw them goodies. But that pigeon looked especially content up there in her hole in the archway. I have no idea what caused the miniature cave in the sandstone. The Siege of Cork, when the abbey tower was a main vantage point during the battle? The sugar refinery fire in 1799? Time? Whatever happened, a member of God's creation found a haven in the ruins.

That fat and happy pigeon reminded me that since the beginning, God has faithfully provided havens of shelter and sustenance for His children. He has opened nests of safety when my life was chaotic and taken part of my life that had fallen into ruin and transformed it into something others could benefit from. And He will continue to.

—*Jeanette Hanscome*

Notes

Notes

LESSON 2: ISAIAH 7:1–21:17; 23:1–18

Isaiah and the Nations

Lord, remind me that You are the One in total control—of the nations and of the happenings in my life. AMEN.

The Crisis of 735–732 BC (7:1–9:7)

In the dark days that preceded World War II, Hitler was gaining power and had convinced himself that he could conquer the world. His forces crossed the Polish frontier shortly before 6 a.m. on September 1, 1939. Europe and much of the outside world soon became involved in a life-and-death struggle that did not end until the Nazis and their allies finally surrendered.

There are many parallels between the situation the world faced in the 1930s and that which confronted Judah and Israel in the 730s BC. The Assyrian Empire was at the height of its power. Led by Tiglath-Pileser III (745–727 BC), its mighty armies terrorized the smaller nations of the Middle East. The prophet Isaiah gives us a graphic description that might well reflect the precision with which the Assyrians marched and fought (5:27–30). Before the eighth century BC ended, they had brought all of Palestine under their control. Consequently, the people of Isaiah's time had ample reason to feel helpless and insecure.

The Sign of Shear-jashub

A coalition of small nations was formed in 735 BC in a vain effort to counteract the Assyrian threat. It was led by Rezin of Damascus and Pekah of Samaria. They also tried to bring Ahaz of Jerusalem into their coalition, but he refused to join them, and in retaliation they launched an attack on Judah (7:1). Their apparent intention was to replace Ahaz with a king who would be more cooperative.

Ahaz was terrified at the prospect of having to face the combined forces of Israel and Syria (7:2). It may have been at this time that he offered his own son in sacrifice (see 2 Kings 16:3), hoping by this act of desperation to avert the wrath of God. This despicable pagan act was a direct violation of God's Word in condemning the practice of child sacrifice spelled out in Deuteronomy 12:29–31.

It was at this point in history that Ahaz had his famous encounter with the prophet Isaiah. It took place when Isaiah was told to take his son Shear-jashub and go out to meet Ahaz "at the end of the aqueduct of the Upper Pool, on the road to the Launderer's Field" (7:3, NIV)—probably an open field area that was used for drying and bleaching cloth. Apparently the king was checking out the water system of Jerusalem in anticipation of the coming siege.

The presence of Isaiah's son on this occasion was certainly not accidental, because God had told the prophet to take him along. His name, Shear-jashub, meant "a remnant shall return." Isaiah's son's name has two possible interpretations. It could be interpreted either as a threat—"*only* a remnant shall return"—or as a promise—"a remnant *shall* return." The reference, of course, was to survivors of the coming holocaust. Shear-jashub, therefore, was a living reminder to Ahaz of the choices God was giving him.

When Isaiah met Ahaz, he tried to persuade the king to trust God alone for deliverance in this crisis (7:4). The prophet's counsel was religiously and politically sound. The only appropriate response to the situation facing Ahaz was faith, not feverish activity and anxiety over the defenses of Jerusalem. Isaiah recognized that the coalition formed by Pekah and Rezin had little chance of succeeding. The term of ridicule he used to describe them was that of "smoking firebrands" (7:4, KJV)—the end of a log that is left after a flame has died down and the log smolders and smokes. Isaiah's description labeled Pekah and Rezin as all smoke and no fire. Once they had been removed, the crisis would be over (7:7–8).

Nothing is said in our scripture lesson about Ahaz's response to Isaiah. However, according to the writer of 2 Kings, he asked Tiglath-Pileser, king of Assyria, to come to his aid (2 Kings 16:7–9). And he used the treasures of the Temple and palace as a payoff for this assistance. Tiglath-Pileser was only too glad to oblige.

Ahaz's request to the king of Assyria to come to his aid was like inviting the fox to guard the henhouse, for he now found himself at the mercy of his "protectors." He had given up his freedom in exchange for security and must now pay whatever price the king of Assyria demanded. This involved not only the loss of political power but also the incorporation of pagan practices into the Temple worship (2 Kings 16:10–18). Ahaz would have been wiser if he had listened to Isaiah and had trusted God rather than man.

The Sign of Immanuel

The prophet invited Ahaz to ask for a sign to prove that the message he had given him was from the Lord (7:10–17). A sign is an occurrence in nature or an event in history that is mysterious and awe-inspiring and has meaning beyond itself. Of the seventy-nine times signs are mentioned in the Old Testament, twenty-five refer to the plagues in Egypt. Old Testament signs never stand alone but are always closely related to a word from the Lord and are given to validate that word. Moses, for example, was allowed to perform signs in order to convince Pharoah that the Lord had indeed commanded him to lead the people of Israel out of Egypt. Signs were given to convince skeptics and to make believers out of scoffers.

Ahaz might have been convinced by a sign, but he refused to ask for one. To have done so would have meant abandoning his own course of action. He pretended his refusal was based on religious principles: he would "not put the LORD to a test" (7:12, NIV). But, of course, that was phony. The real reason was that he had already made up his mind to appeal to Tiglath-Pileser, and he resented the prophet's meddling in his affairs. We all tend to reject advice, even good advice, when we have already made up our minds.

Isaiah then announced that God would give a sign, even if Ahaz didn't ask for it (7:14). The prophet said that a child would be born and would be given a symbolic name. That name, Immanuel, meaning "God with us," would be a sign of God's abiding presence with His people in their time of crisis. Before the child was old enough to choose between good and evil, perhaps at his twelfth birthday, the two lands now threatening Judah would both be kingless (7:16). This prophecy was strikingly fulfilled when Tiglath-Pileser invaded Israel in 733 BC (see 2 Kings 15:29–30) and destroyed Damascus soon thereafter.

Since the birth of Immanuel was to be a sign to Ahaz of the defeat of the two kings threatening him, we must decide who Immanuel was. Was he the son of Ahaz, of Isaiah, or perhaps of some unnamed person? The fact that his mother is called "*the* young woman" (with the definite article "the" in Hebrew, which is reflected in most Bible translations) suggests that she was well known and therefore most likely the wife of Ahaz.

The traditional Jewish interpretation is that verse 14 points to the birth of Hezekiah. This suggests that the prophecy of his birth was meant to be a messianic prophecy and should be compared to similar prophecies in Isaiah 9:1–7; 11:1–9; Micah 5:2–6; and Zechariah 9:9–10. Isaiah, faced with the stubborn unbelief of Ahaz, foretold God's provision of a more worthy heir to the throne of David.

From the wording of our scripture lesson, it is clear that the prophet expected this to occur during his own lifetime. He could not foresee that the coming of the One who finally fulfilled the Immanuel prophecy would be delayed for another seven centuries. The prophecy was transposed in Christian tradition to a higher key in its fulfillment in the birth of Jesus Christ, who also was called "Immanuel . . . God with us" (Matthew 1:23). In Him the promise of God's presence was fulfilled in ways that even Isaiah was unable to anticipate.

Bitter Fruits of a Bad Policy

Ahaz regarded Isaiah's advice to trust God as totally unrealistic. He preferred to put his trust in Tiglath-Pileser. That decision proved to be very costly. It set the stage for a century of Assyrian domination of the land of Judah (7:18–25).

Isaiah forewarned Ahaz of what would happen because of his decision. The prophet predicted that because of the shortsighted policies of Ahaz, Judah would become a battlefield, with the armies of Egypt and Assyria converging upon her (7:18–20). As a result of continued warfare, the land of Judah would be stripped of all but the barest essentials and its people would be forced to live like desert nomads (7:21–22). The land itself would revert to briars and thorns and would be fit only for hunting or for the grazing of stray flocks of sheep and cattle (7:24–25). Stupidity has always been a poor substitute for sound foreign policy.

The Sign of Maher-shalal-hash-baz

As we move ahead to chapter 8, we see that once again the prophet foretold the coming downfall of Syria (Damascus) and Israel (Samaria) by the Assyrians (8:1–4). This time his prediction was given in an unusual manner. He took a large tablet and, in the presence of reliable witnesses, wrote on it a kind of coded message. It read, "To Maher-shalal-hash-baz." The literal translation of this Hebrew word was "The spoil speeds; the prey hastes." It was a prediction of doom for Syria and Israel and a message of hope for Judah and the house of Ahaz.

The prophet then slept with his wife, and she conceived and bore a son who was named Maher-shalal-hash-baz. His birth, like that of Immanuel, was to serve as a sign of the imminent destruction of Syria and Israel. And before the child was old enough to say simple words like *mother* and *father*, the two nations menacing Judah would be captured and plundered by the king of Assyria (8:4).

The Message of the Two Rivers

The birth and naming of Maher-shalal-hash-baz was meant to awaken faith on the part of King Ahaz and the people of Jerusalem. But it didn't work that way, as the king was stubbornly determined to follow his own counsel.

Having failed twice to persuade Ahaz to put trust and confidence in God, Isaiah predicted coming judgment. He did this by using the analogy of two rivers. One was called Shiloah, and we are told that its waters flowed "gently" (Isaiah 8:6, NIV). Shiloah has been identified as a small trench or aqueduct that carried water from the Gihon Spring to a reservoir inside Jerusalem. The other river was a symbol of Assyria and quite likely referred to the Euphrates. Its waters are described as "mighty and many" (verse 7, ESV).

As the prophet colorfully pictured what was to come, he accused the people of Judah of rejecting the flowing waters of Shiloah—another way of saying they had refused God's offer of help. Because of their disobedience, the waters of a mighty and rushing river, here identified as the king of Assyria, would overflow its banks and inundate their land (8:7–8).

This scene reminds us of the poignant words in the Gospel of Luke, "As [Jesus] approached Jerusalem and saw the city, he wept over it and said, 'If you, even you, had only known on this day what would bring you peace—but now it is hidden from your eyes'" (19:41–42, NIV).

The Fear of God and the Fear of Man

This next movement in our scripture lesson (8:9–18) is also related to the crisis of 735 BC. Here God issues a warning to the prophet himself. He is commanded to stand firmly against the wave of fear that prevailed in Judah (8:11–12). Instead, he was to put his fear and trust in God. In doing that, he would have no reason to fear anything (8:13). In response to the word of the Lord, Isaiah said, "I will wait for the Lord . . . I will wait eagerly for Him" (8:17, NASB). What a magnificent state of obedience and commitment! And what a superb model for us in our times of crisis.

Light Shines in the Darkness

The prophet leads us now to a picture of vivid contrasts—darkness and light (8:19–9:7). First, he describes a time when darkness and anguish overwhelmed the people of Zebulun and Naphtali (8:21–9:1). These were the two northern-most tribes of Israel, and they would have borne the brunt of Tiglath-Pileser's invasion of the land around 733 BC (see 2 Kings 15:29). The desperate plight of those who fled the invader is vividly described by Isaiah as he pictures them searching for food, cursing their king for allowing this to happen and God for having seemingly abandoned them. Wherever they looked there was "distress and darkness, the gloom of anguish; and they will be driven away into darkness" (8:22, NASB). It was a desperate and grim picture!

Then suddenly the scene changes. Those who once walked in darkness have now seen a great light (9:2). The sharp contrast between the prophet's earlier words (8:21–22) and these words reminds us of the first light of creation that broke upon the primeval chaos in the beginning of time (see Genesis 1:1–5).

The people who were delivered from darkness and anguish now celebrate (9:3). Their joy is compared to that of farmers bringing in the harvest, or to soldiers dividing the spoil after victory is won. Two reasons are given for their celebration. First, their oppressors have been defeated and their time of servitude has ended (9:4). Second, the weapons of war lie abandoned on the battlefield and remain only to be gathered and burned (9:5). All of this signals a new time of peace.

And what had brought about this sudden change? It is the word that a child had been born—a child destined to become king (9:6–7). But it is instantly clear that he wouldn't be like the kings that had ruled over Israel and Judah. The names the prophet gives this new king are most descriptive: "Wonderful, Counsellor, The mighty God, The everlasting Father, The Prince of Peace" (9:6, KJV). This reign, unlike that of the kings that Isaiah had to put up with, would be a reign of peace and justice. The word "peace" means more than the mere absence of hostility. It describes the rich, harmonious, and joy-filled life of all of God's people.

Who was this child so divinely endowed? Jewish tradition identifies him with Hezekiah, the son of Ahaz. But while the prophet may have hoped that Hezekiah would establish a reign of peace and justice, his hopes were never realized. In fact, by the end of Hezekiah's reign, the land of Judah had been devastated by the armies of Assyria (Isaiah 1:7–8; 36:1).

These hopeful words remind us of a Child who was born long after Isaiah and in whom these words were finally fulfilled. The Child of Bethlehem was the long-awaited Messiah, the King of the Jews, the Prince of Peace, the Savior of all humankind. It is this Child who changed the shape of history and brought peace to all who believe—through His life, death, and resurrection!

God's Hand of Punishment (9:8–10:4)

Futile Punishment

God in various ways had punished Israel as a nation for its sin, but unfortunately the people had not turned from their sinful ways. This simply meant that they were plunging ahead toward destruction that would become final with the fall of Samaria in 722 BC.

Preliminary disasters had failed to shake the confidence of the people in their ability to defend themselves. Even when part of their city was destroyed, they set about rebuilding it with better materials (9:9–10). They improved their building methods but not their morals, and Isaiah makes it clear they made no effort to seek the Lord (9:13). He further says that their leaders led them astray (9:14–16).

Fiery Judgment

With strong and colorful language Isaiah describes the chaos that existed in the northern kingdom of Israel during the closing years of its history (9:18–21). From the death of Jeroboam II in 746 BC (2 Kings 14:29) until the fall of Samaria in 722 BC

(2 Kings 17:5–6), Israel had six kings in rapid succession. It was a time when successive wannabes and pretenders to the throne tried to be king, and not one of them was qualified for the job.

The threat facing the people of Israel is described as a fire burning on two fronts. On the one hand, their wickedness, burning like a forest fire out of control, was threatening to consume them (9:18). On the other hand, the wrath of God was also kindled against them (9:19). At the same time, the nation was plagued by internal strife and civil warfare (9:20–21).

Let Judah Also Take Warning

Next, when Isaiah refers to "the poor of my people" (10:2, KJV), we know that the prophet has now directed his attention to the southern kingdom of Judah. His warning is clear: God will hold them accountable for their sins. Isaiah refers specifically to the sin of depriving the poor—the widows and orphans—of their legal rights (10:1–2). Furthermore, the prophet predicts their day of reckoning will come—they would either be killed in battle or carried off into captivity (10:3–4).

Assyria, the Instrument of God's Anger (10:5–34)

We come now to the severest crisis of Isaiah's ministry as a prophet. We described this in lesson 1 as Isaiah's fourth crisis. This was the occasion of King Hezekiah's rebellion against the might of the Assyrian Empire. In response to Hezekiah's revolt, Sennacherib stormed through Judah and put Jerusalem under siege. This was a time of severe hardship and suffering for the people of Judah and Jerusalem, but relief finally came when the Lord intervened and the Assyrian army lifted the siege and the people were spared further hardship and suffering.

But, tragically, their miraculous relief did not bring the people to the place of repenting of their sin. While they staged a grand celebration over being spared, they did not turn to the Lord. As Isaiah reflected on all that had happened, he apparently pondered the dilemma of how God could use a wicked and perverse people like the Assyrians to punish His chosen people. Out of these reflections seems to have come what might be called Isaiah's philosophy. This philosophy is expressed in this part of our scripture lesson.

Isaiah's Philosophy of History

Isaiah never doubted that God was in control of all of history and that this control extended to the entire world. On the other hand, Isaiah lived at a time when the Assyrians were at the zenith of their power. Their armed forces, like those of Hitler's in World War II, were able for a time to overcome everything in their way. On the surface it seemed that God was on the run, and history was being shaped by the Assyrian forces.

But that's not the way Isaiah saw it. He believed that history was not governed by chance or by the Assyrian military might. He was firmly convinced that God was merely using the Assyrians to discipline His people (10:5–6).

At the same time, Isaiah was aware that the Assyrians did not see themselves as serving the purposes of God. They were simply bent on world conquest and the pursuit of self-glory (10:7). Like all dictators before and since, they were drunk on their own power and loudly boasted of their successes on the field of battle (10:8–14).

It was not Isaiah's intention to excuse the Assyrians for their cruelty or to praise them for unknowingly serving the purposes of God. Instead, he rebuked them for their excessive pride when he asked, "Does the ax raise itself above the person who swings it, or the saw boast against the one who uses it?" (10:15, NIV). Furthermore, Isaiah announced that when the Lord had finished using Assyria to punish the people of Jerusalem, He would then judge Assyria and remove all their reasons for boasting (10:12, 16–19).

Next comes the assurance that after the proud and arrogant Assyrians had moved off the stage of history, the Lord's chosen people would be secure (10:24–27). The Lord's chastening and discipline was only meant to cleanse them and to prepare them for the future.

The Bible teaches that the Lord disciplines us when we disobey Him, and He does this for our benefit so that we might become more like Him (see Hebrews 12:6–11). We probably resist the Lord's discipline as much as the Israelites did, but in our better moments we know that His actions are motivated by His love for us and that He understands our needs better than we do.

The Reign of the Messiah (11:1–16)

In our lesson so far, we have looked at two magnificent statements that speak of the Messiah: His birth (7:14) and His coronation as King (9:1–7). Now we come to the third statement that describes His reign of righteousness and justice (11:1–9).

The Divinely Endowed Messiah

The prophet now gives one of the most exalted portrayals of the Messiah in the Old Testament (11:1–9). We are told that He would emerge as a "shoot . . . from the stump of Jesse" (11:1, NIV). This means that the Messiah was to be a descendant of Jesse, the father of David. But it also means that He would not appear until the tree of Jesse had been cut down and only a stump remained—until the line of Davidic kings had ceased to exist. We know that this happened when Jerusalem was destroyed in 587 BC and the last reigning king was exiled to Babylon. None of the earlier kings of Judah had lived up to God's expectations, but now there would be a new beginning.

Isaiah announced that the coming King would be endowed with the Spirit of the Lord (11:2). In the Old Testament there are numerous accounts telling how God gave His Spirit to certain men and women so that they might perform assigned tasks with greater skill. For example, the gift of the Spirit to certain Israelites in the wilderness gave them the necessary skill to make fine works of gold, silver, brass, precious stones, and carved wood for the Tabernacle (Exodus 35:30–35). The gift of the Spirit inspired other persons to function as prophets (see Numbers 11:29; 24:2; 2 Chronicles 24:20; Ezekiel 11:5; Joel 2:28–29), others as judges (see Judges 3:10; 6:34; 11:29), and still others as kings (1 Samuel 11:6; 16:13). Consequently, it should not surprise us that the Messianic King would also be endowed with God's Spirit.

Six specific gifts of the Spirit are mentioned here. The first pair, wisdom and understanding, stress Messiah's wisdom. The second pair, counsel and might, speak of His administrative skill. And the third pair, knowledge and fear of the Lord, refer to His piety. This reminds us that the Spirit of God descended upon Jesus at His baptism (Matthew 3:16), and that He began His ministry in Nazareth by announcing He had been anointed by the Spirit of the Lord in order to accomplish His mission (Luke 4:18).

Rendering True Judgment

Traditionally, Israel's kings served also as judges (see 2 Samuel 15:1–4; 1 Kings 3:16–28; 2 Kings 6:24–31). They were charged with the responsibility of executing justice and righteousness, especially on behalf of the homeless, the poor, and the oppressed (see 1 Kings 10:9; Jeremiah 22:1–5). But Isaiah announced that this would change when the Messiah took His throne. He would not judge on the basis of outward appearance but on the basis of a person's true character (11:3). He would be fair in His execution of justice and would deliver the poor from those who oppressed them (11:4–5).

The Transformation of Nature

But that's not all! The prophet now describes with colorful imagery what it will be like in the natural world when the Messiah comes (11:6–9). This great restoration is described as a return to the ideal state that existed when Adam and Eve occupied the Garden of Eden (see also Isaiah 65:17–25; Ezekiel 34:25–28; 47:6–12; Joel 3:18; Amos 9:13–15). The original harmony of nature had been destroyed because of sin (see Genesis 3:14–19). Now Isaiah spoke of a time when the coming Messiah would restore this harmony (11:6–8; see also

Romans 8:19–23). Then there would be peaceful coexistence between all living creatures—animals as well as humans. The rule of life then would be that no living being would act in a manner so as to hurt or destroy another living being (11:9).

And when would all of this happen? The prophet answers that it would happen when "the earth will be full of the knowledge of the LORD as the waters cover the sea" (11:9, NASB). What a glad day that will be!

The Homecoming of the Exiles

Continuing the messianic theme, Isaiah looks ahead to that time when all dispersed and displaced persons "from the islands of the sea" and "from the four corners of the earth" (11:11–12, NASB) shall return to their rightful place, and this includes those exiled from Israel in 722 BC and from Judah in 587 BC.

The one who would bring all these exiles home from distant lands is identified as "the root of Jesse" (11:10, KJV). Here the word "root" seems to be a technical term for the Messiah. Isaiah uses the same word later to describe the Servant of the Lord as "a root out of dry ground" (53:2, NIV; see also Revelation 22:16). The one called the "root of Jesse" is a "signal" (ESV) or a "banner" (NIV) not only to the dispersed Jews but also to the Gentiles (11:10, 12). The words used here picture a flagstaff set up on a battlefield in order to serve as a rallying point for scattered troops. Here it refers to the rallying of both Jews and Gentiles behind the Messianic King, a theme mentioned often in the Bible (see Psalm 72:8–11; Isaiah 49:5–6; Micah 5:4; Zechariah 9:9–10; Revelation 11:15).

The Exodus theme is also picked up in these verses. This explains the reference to the Lord's acting a "second time" (11:11) to recover the remnant of His people from the nations; the first time would have been their rescue from Egypt. But this time their exodus would be from Assyrian oppression. Even the nations listed in verse 14 are the same as those the people of Israel encountered at the time of their first entry into Canaan. And this time, too, the Lord would provide a "highway," as virtually all Bible versions translate the word—a way of escape—even as He had at the time of the first Exodus (11:16). While Isaiah's prophecy here is composed of some rather complicated imagery, the central truth remains constant in all time. God has provided a way of salvation for His people through Christ, who is the way, the truth, and the life.

Two Hymns of Praise (12:1–6)

After the people of Israel had been delivered from Pharoah's army at the Red Sea, they celebrated their deliverance with a hymn of praise (Exodus 15:1–18). Now Isaiah looks ahead to an even greater deliverance that inspires a new hymn of praise from the people. This is expressed in the two brief hymns that make up our scripture lesson now and that form the conclusion to the first major portion of the book of Isaiah.

Praise for Great Deliverance

The first hymn (12:1–3) begins with the words, "In that day you will say . . ." (NIV). Then follows the magnificent affirmation in verse 2, "Surely God is my salvation; I will trust and not be afraid. The LORD, the LORD himself, is my strength and my defense; he has become my salvation" (NIV). Here we see that in framing this hymn, the prophet has drawn from the poetic grandeur of the Exodus writer (15:2) and from the Psalmist (Psalm 118:14, 21).

The hymn speaks of a time when the Lord was angry with His people, but that is followed immediately with the assurance that He is no longer angry—He is now their salvation. This is the first of many occurrences of the important word *salvation* in the book of Isaiah (see 25:9; 49:6; 52:7, 10). *Salvation* comes from a verb root meaning "to be wide" or spacious and expresses the idea that salvation or victory is whole and complete for the people of God.

Praise for the Great Deliverer

In the second of the two brief hymns, praise is offered to God for His wonderful actions toward and for His people (12:4–5). And the hymn closes in praise that God is with them (12:6)—the "Holy One of Israel" is with them. These words leap the centuries to the promise of Jesus to the faithful in all time, "Lo, I am with you always, even unto the end of the world" (Matthew 28:20, KJV). That is a *wide* and *spacious* promise!

Prophecies against the Nations (13:1–19:15; 20:1–21:17; 23:1–18)

There are collections of foreign prophecies in almost all the prophetic books of the Old Testament. As a rule, these prophecies are directed against the foreign nations and are condemnatory because of their gross pagan and sinful practices. For this reason, they are frequently introduced by a Hebrew word that is rendered variously as "burden" (KJV), "pronouncement" (NASB), "prophecy" (NIV), and "oracle" (ESV). This Hebrew term is used ten times to introduce foreign prophecies in this section of Isaiah (13:1; 14:28; 15:1; 17:1; 19:1; 21:1, 11, 13; 22:1; 23:1). This means that these are all doom prophecies directed against the enemies of Israel and Judah who had rejected God.

There are other prophecies against the foreign pagan nations scattered throughout the book of Isaiah, but this is the most extensive collection of such prophecies. The scattered foreign prophecies are addressed to Edom (34:1–17; 63:1–6), Assyria (37:21–29), and Babylon (47:1–15). But these collected prophecies are addressed to Babylon (13:1–14:23; 21:1–10), Assyria (14:24–27), Philistia (14:28–32), Moab (15:1–16:14), Damascus (Syria) (17:1–6), Ethiopia (18:1–17), Egypt (19:1–5; 20:1–6), Edom (21:11–12), and the Phoenician cities of Tyre and Sidon (23:1–12).

These prophecies are related to events in the history of Israel and Judah stretching from 735 to at least 587 BC. In other words, they cover the entire time span of the book of Isaiah, including the years of Exile. However, they do not seem to be arranged in any special chronological order. For example, the prophecies against Babylon are not placed together in the collection, as one would have expected in a chronological arrangement.

The Doom of Babylon

The prophecies against Babylon are combined here for ease of treatment (13:1–14:23; 21:1–10). Nabopolassar, the king of Babylon, fought and won his independence from Assyria in 626 BC. From that date until 539 BC, when the Babylonian Empire was conquered by Cyrus the Great of Persia, Babylon's influence was dominant throughout the Middle East.

The prophecies against Babylon should be dated somewhere between 626 and 539 BC, the period that marked the height of its power. With colorful imagery the prophet describes Babylon as "the glory of kingdoms, the splendor and pomp of the Chaldeans" (13:19, ESV). Because of the cruelty shown those who opposed Babylon, it is called "the treacherous one" and "the destroyer" (21:2, NASB). And the king is described as "the man that made the earth to tremble, that did shake kingdoms" (14:16, KJV).

Babylon is mentioned first in the foreign prophecies not because it was the earliest of Israel's enemies but because it was among the most hated. The armies of Babylon were responsible for the destruction of Jerusalem in 587 BC and for deporting Judah's leading citizens to exile. Jews came to regard Babylon as the archetype of all their foes. This helps to explain why Babylon is sometimes used as a symbol for Rome in the New Testament (see 1 Peter 5:13; Revelation 14:8; 16:19; 17:5).

The message of these oracles is that God places a limit on the power of tyrants, even tyrants as strong as Babylon. First, Isaiah foresees a mighty army being assembled (13:1–5) that would utterly destroy Babylon with a fury that defied description (13:6–16). Here the Medes are credited with conquering

Babylon (13:17; 21:2), but it remained for Cyrus, the conqueror of the Medes, to carry out this threat. The completeness of the devastation of the once mighty Babylon is colorfully described by the prophet (13:19–22). He pictures the once proud country as becoming the haunt of wild beasts, howling creatures, ostriches and owls (NASB), and wild goats (13:21). Babylon was finally and totally destroyed by the Parthians in 127 BC and, at the beginning of the Christian era, was inhabited only by a small group of astronomers and mathematicians.

Special attention is paid to the downfall of Babylon's tyrant king (14:4–23). We read that his death would be cause for celebration (14:5–8), and he would be given a special reception when he arrived at Sheol (14:9). In the Old Testament, Sheol refers to the resting place of the dead. It is sometimes rendered "hell," but it should not be confused with the Greek word *gehenna,* which refers to a place of eternal punishment.

The prophet then goes on to elaborate in colorful and descriptive language the plight of the Babylonian king in Sheol (14:10–20). The once exalted, high-and-mighty king of Babylon would be "brought down" to "the far reaches of the pit" (14:15, ESV). The Babylon prophecy ends with a prayer that the tyrant-king wouldn't have any survivors to continue his dynasty (14:15–20).

The Destruction of Assyria

Next comes the brief prophecy against Assyria. It is likely that Isaiah spoke these words on the occasion of Sennacherib's invasion of Judah in 701 BC (see Isaiah 36–37). It is so similar in style and content to the anti-Assyrian prophecy given earlier (10:5–34) that many believe these two prophecies belong together. Again, we are given a vivid illustration of the eternal truth that the long-term events of history are determined by God's purposes and not by the power of mighty nations like Assyria (14:24, 27).

Warning to Philistia

In the year that King Ahaz died (14:28), the Lord warned the people of Philistia not to pin their hopes on an early end to the Assyrian occupation and domination of their land. It is suggested in verse 29 that the death of the Assyrian king may have raised hopes that this would happen. But they were warned that even though the serpent—the Assyrian king—may have died, there was no reason to suppose that a revolt against Assyria would be successful. Just such a revolt occurred in 711 BC, led by the ruler of the city-state of Ashdod. Isaiah was bitterly opposed to Judah's joining this revolt. He was firmly convinced that the people of Judah should put their faith in God and not in foreign alliances.

The Doom of Moab

The prophet next turns his attention toward Moab, a neighboring country just east of the Dead Sea (15:1–16:14). The Moabites were descendants of Lot and, because of this, were related to the Israelites. There were periods of time in their history when friendly relations existed between the two countries (such as in the book of Ruth), and there were other times when they were extremely hostile toward each other. This accounts for the mood of the prophecy, which at times seems sympathetic and at other times seems adversarial.

Most of this part of our scripture lesson concerns an invasion of Moab by an unidentified enemy who is wreaking havoc on the land. Both the date and the circumstances surrounding this invasion are very hazy and uncertain because of our lack of detailed information about Moabite history. To Isaiah's first listeners and readers it is likely that the prophecy regarding Moab had meaning, because the situation and events of the time might have been familiar to them, but for us it is virtually impossible to come up with an interpretation of this obscure passage.

The Doom of Damascus

From Moab to the south and east, Isaiah now focuses the spotlight of his attention on Damascus (Syria) to the north (17:1–6). In reality, though, the light of time is also shining on Israel, referred to here as Ephraim (17:3) and Jacob (17:4). It is quite generally agreed that this prophecy is related to the crisis of 735–734 BC when the kings of Damascus and the northern kingdom of Israel were allied against the southern kingdom of Judah (see 7:1–8:4; 9:8–21).

Here Isaiah predicts the downfall of both Damascus (17:1–2) and Israel (17:3–5). The prophet employs vivid imagery, as with three different figures of speech he describes the devastation of Israel. First he describes that devastation as being like wasting away, a body loss of flesh and fat (17:4). Then he compares it to the reaping of fields of grain (17:5), and finally, like the gleanings that are left behind after the grape and olive harvest (17:6). The picture is one of complete destruction for both Damascus and the northern kingdom of Israel. Undoubtedly, the prophet was referring to the invasion of both Syria and Israel by Tiglath-Pileser III of Assyria around 732 BC.

The Folly of Serving Handmade Gods

Between Isaiah's prophecies against Damascus and concerning Ethiopia and Egypt, he issues a plea for authentic worship of God instead of worship of the handmade pagan gods or the foreign gods of vegetation (17:7–11). In other words, they were to worship the one true God who was the Creator of all things—they were not to worship that which He had created.

The Roar of the Nations

The prophet then speaks of "the thunder of many peoples" and "the roar of nations" (17:12–14, ESV). In a few words the point is made that even though hostile forces—of whatever kind—threaten the people of God, they are assured of deliverance. "He will rebuke them, and they will flee far away, and be chased like chaff on the mountains before the wind, or like whirling dust before a gale" (17:13, NASB). Here is a powerful affirmation for God's people in all time that in spite of the fury in the days of Isaiah or in our time today, God is in charge; He is the Lord of history, and our faith is secure in Him.

Condemnation of Ethiopia and Egypt

Isaiah next turns his attention to the south—to Ethiopia and Egypt (18:1–19:15; 20:1–6). The book of Isaiah refers to Ethiopia and Egypt almost as if they were synonymous terms. This was because Egypt was ruled by an Ethiopian dynasty (the twenty-fifth dynasty) from 715 until 663 BC. During this dynasty there was a revival of Egyptian power, raising the hopes of the Pharoahs that they might regain control of Palestine from the Assyrians. This accounts for Egypt's frequent attempts to meddle in the affairs of Judah during this period. Any hopes that Egypt might have had to reassert her influence over Palestine were dashed, however, when the Assyrians launched an attack in 663 BC and destroyed the Egyptian capital city of Thebes (see Nahum 3:8–10).

In this part of our scripture lesson Isaiah speaks of the arrival in Jerusalem of an Ethiopian (Egyptian) delegation seeking to enlist Judah's king in a coalition against Assyria (18:1–7). The most likely date for this occurrence would be around 715 BC. In a polite but firm way, Isaiah advised the foreigners to leave Jerusalem and return to their own land (18:1–2). Then in verse 7 the prophet looks ahead to the time when the Assyrian crisis would have passed and Ethiopians would come up to Mount Zion—Jerusalem—to pay homage to the Lord of hosts (see also Acts 8:27–28).

Next, Isaiah speaks of the coming judgment on Egypt, and he does so in three descriptive stanzas of a poem (19:1–5). The first stanza pictures the civil strife that rocked Egypt when it was invaded (19:1–2). While Isaiah does not identify the invading forces, their leader is described as "a hard master" and "a fierce king" (19:3–4, ESV), and we're told that the Egyptians pleaded with their pagan gods for help.

The second stanza (19:5–10) describes the drying up of the Nile River and the complete collapse of the Egyptian economy. Egypt depended upon the Nile for its very existence.

Without it the country would have been nothing more than an eastward extension of the great Sahara Desert.

The third stanza (19:11–15) describes the inability of Egypt's leaders to remedy the situation. In colorful language the prophet sees the Egyptian wise men as stupid and ineffective, and their nobility as fools (19:11–13). There was no help for a nation governed by such weak leadership (19:15).

Isaiah's Dramatic Act

A highly symbolic act of the prophet Isaiah is described in the first six verses of chapter 20. This oracle is dated in 711 BC, the year in which Sargon, king of Assyria, captured the Philistine city of Ashdod (20:1). For the three years before that climactic event, Isaiah had walked the streets of Jerusalem "naked and barefoot" (20:2–3, NASB). He did this to dramatize the fate that awaited Egypt and Ethiopia at the hands of Assyria (20:3–4) and to convince Hezekiah and the people of Judah of the futility of trusting in Egypt or any other foreign power for protection (20:5–6). His efforts apparently were successful, for there is no record that Sargon took any punitive action against Jerusalem at this time.

Restored to God's Favor (19:16–25; 21:11–17; 23:1–18)

The remaining prophecies against the pagan Near Eastern nations include those pronounced against Edom (21:11–12) and the Phoenician coastal cities of Tyre and Sidon (23:1–12).

We note that, interspersed with the words of judgment against the foreign powers, there are also words of comfort and hope. We see in this a reminder that God's final word is not one of judgment but of redemption. Leaping across the centuries, the New Testament writer picked up on this when he wrote, "The Lord is not slow about His promise, as some count slowness, but is patient toward you, *not willing for any to perish, but for all to come to repentance*" (2 Peter 3:9, NASB; italics added for emphasis).

Hope for Egypt and Assyria

The first message of hope concerns Egypt and Assyria (19:16–25). This is a surprising message for two reasons. First, Egypt and Assyria were the two nations most feared and hated by the people of Israel and Judah during Isaiah's lifetime. Second, Isaiah not only announced pardon for the past sins of Egypt and Assyria, but he also predicted that they would become converted and be active worshippers of the Lord God. It is thought this prophecy looked ahead to that time when there was strong Jewish influence in Egypt proper. And this particular prophecy is considered to be the most universal in Hebrew prophetic literature.

Hope for Tyre

The second message of hope concerns the city-state of Tyre, located on the Mediterranean coast in what is today southern Lebanon (23:13–18). Tyre prospered greatly from its fleets of merchant ships that plied the Mediterranean. Isaiah first predicted a seventy-year interruption of Tyre's sea trade caused by an attack from the Chaldeans (23:13–16). Then he predicted a revival of Tyre's commercial activity after those seventy years, using the metaphor of a prostitute returning to her trade (23:17). The prophet went out of his way to say that "the Lord will deal with Tyre," which "will ply her trade with all the kingdoms on the face of the earth" (NIV). This prostitution imagery seems to us like a strange metaphor for the prophet to use, but he apparently meant nothing more than that Tyre would be permitted to renew her world "lucrative . . . trade." Isaiah even affirms that the profits from Tyre's "profit and her earnings" (23:18, NIV) would be consecrated—set apart—to the Lord, providing "abundant food and fine clothes" for His people. He may have expected that the restored city of Tyre would come to worship the Lord, although he does not say so.

Conclusion

The chapters covered by this lesson are not always easy to understand. Since so many centuries separate us from the time of Isaiah, we have difficulty identifying the many nations referred to and understanding how they were related to the history of Israel and Judah. It is easy to get lost as we try to work our way through this rather long section of Isaiah's prophecies.

At this point, you might even be asking yourself if it is worth the effort to try to understand obscure prophecies like these. There are two reasons it is worth the effort.

First, we are reminded here that God created all the nations of the world, not just the people of Israel and Judah. Actually, the Israelites were chosen by God, not so that other nations would be excluded from His plan for the world, but it was God's will that all the nations of the world would be included. Israel was just the pilot project in God's grand design to bring

His blessing of salvation to everyone. The carrying out of that plan took place in two major steps. The first was the call and commission of Abraham to be a blessing to all nations (Genesis 12:1–3). And the second was the sending of God's own Son to be the Savior of people in all time.

Second, we learn here that God holds all of the nations of the world accountable for their actions. We are accustomed to think in terms of individual responsibility and may easily overlook the fact that there is such a thing as collective responsibility. Groups as well as individuals are responsible for their actions.

In Jesus's parable of the last judgment (Matthew 25:31–46) we get a vivid picture of group responsibility for the world's poor, homeless, sick, and enslaved. We do not live and serve God in isolation.

Then, too, in Isaiah's time and ours we see that God, in His own way, condemns those nations who employ military might to impose their will on weaker countries. The history of the last hundred-plus years is full of illustrations of major world powers that have arrogantly attacked neighboring countries in their lust to dominate. For a time they may have seemed to succeed, but in God's time justice has had its way.

The prophet Isaiah is a constant reminder to us that, though there is most certainly evil and injustice in the world, the Lord God of history—our God—is in charge.

God, I can rejoice because, despite everything going on around me, You are in charge! Amen.

INSPIRATION FROM THE BOOK OF ISAIAH

And the Spirit of the Lord shall rest upon him, the Spirit of wisdom and understanding, the Spirit of counsel and might, the Spirit of knowledge and the fear of the Lord.

—Isaiah 11:2 (ESV)

Over the past year or two, I found myself praying the same prayer over and over: "Lord, what should I do?" My husband's real-estate career was hitting some major bumps because of the economy. I wondered if, instead of writing books and doing freelance editing, I should venture into the corporate world—that mysterious place where writing is called "communications" and jobs came with that magical extra, "benefits."

For a few months, I applied for jobs that I didn't really want, hoping somehow my husband's career would turn around, or he'd find another job. I wondered how my working long hours in a corporate job would impact my kids, who still needed me. I wondered, *What is the best thing to do? Which way should I go?*

Gradually, it dawned on me: I have access to Jesus, who has wisdom, understanding, counsel, strength, and knowledge. Rather than complain to Him about my situation, I needed to seek out that wisdom and counsel, which He'd made available to me. Jesus not only understood but also had wise counsel to offer me.

When I prayed and asked Him to speak to me, and then became quiet enough to listen, He led me away from my search for a corporate job, at least for now. I continue to write books and edit, but He also provided two part-time jobs with very small companies, where I use my creativity and skills and have incredibly flexible hours. I'm working hard, helping to provide for my family, in a way that fits who I am.

—Keri Wyatt Kent

Notes

Notes

Messages of Judgment and Hope

God, I can trust in Your judgments because I know You judge justly. Amen.

A Prophet's Disappointment in His People (22:1–14)

The most likely setting for this part of our scripture lesson is Jerusalem just after it had been saved from being destroyed by Sennacherib of Assyria in the crisis of 701 BC (see 1:5–9; 10:28–31; 36:1–37:38). Isaiah was an old man by this time, having already spent about forty years as a prophet (see 6:1). In fact, the words here may very well have been among his last recorded messages prior to his death. If so, it shows his bitter disappointment at the way the people of Jerusalem and Judah celebrated their narrow escape from destruction.

Shouting from the Housetops

Once Sennacherib's forces withdrew from Jerusalem, the people staged a kind of Fourth of July celebration (22:1–4). There must have been dancing in the streets and shouting upon the housetops (22:1–2). The flat tops of the houses in Bible times normally served as gathering places for social events. Victory celebrations like this can easily get out of hand, and this seems to have happened in Isaiah's day. The old prophet witnessed with a heavy heart the wild abandon of the crowds. Now, all he asked was to be left alone so he might weep over the destruction of his people (22:3–4).

A City under Siege

In these next verses Isaiah seems to be reflecting on all that led up to this day of celebration (22:5–11). He thought of the hardships the city had experienced while it was under siege by Sennacherib's army, which included recruits from Elam and Kir (22:5–6). Once again, he saw the chariots and horsemen that filled the valleys surrounding the city (22:7), while inside the city itself the people stockpiled weapons, repaired and fortified the city wall, and took steps to safeguard their water supply (22:8–11). But Isaiah condemned their frantic activities as an indication of distrust in God (verse 11).

A Time for Weeping

We next learn that the Lord had given the people of Jerusalem instructions to observe a time of mourning when the Assyrian siege was over (22:12), as one would normally do when a family member had died. It is possible that Isaiah had relayed those instructions himself, but the people ignored the Lord's message, choosing instead to enter into a time of joyous celebration and feasting, saying, "Let us eat and drink, for tomorrow we die" (22:13, ESV). In response to their disobedience the prophet was instructed to say, "'Surely this iniquity will not be atoned for you until you die,' says the Lord God of hosts" (22:14, ESV). Because of the strong and condemnatory language used here, some have called this verse the most pessimistic of all Isaiah's prophecies.

An Overambitious Politician (22:15–25)

We come now to an intriguing scene as the prophet gives us some insight into the arrogant behavior of an overambitious official in the Judean government. We can't help but smile at this scenario because all too often our newspapers describe the downfall of national or state officials who have employed questionable behavior in order to enhance their own self interests. The official's name was Shebna, and he seems to have been chief steward in the palace of the king (22:15)—a position that would have given him considerable authority and prestige (see Genesis 45:8). Next we're told that Shebna, in order to enhance his reputation, decided to hew out a rock tomb and set up a monument to himself, perhaps on the Mount of Olives overlooking Jerusalem (22:16).

But one day as Shebna was supervising this work he received a surprise visit from Isaiah. The prophet looked around and asked, with obvious sarcasm in his voice, "What are you doing here and who gave you permission to cut out a grave for yourself here, hewing your grave on the height and chiseling your resting place in the rock?" (22:16, NIV).

In short, Isaiah is saying, "Why build a monument and a grave here?" Then he tells Shebna that he will be exiled to a foreign country and be buried there instead (22:17–18). But that isn't all the bad news. Isaiah goes on to tell Shebna that he will lose his coveted position, and another official named Eliakim will take his place (22:19–25). Undoubtedly, there's more to the story than Isaiah has given us here. But he has made his point—an insatiable lust for prestige and power results in displacement and exile. It was true in the time of Isaiah, and it is true today as it was then.

An Announcement of Judgment (24:1–20)

We looked at the prophetic judgment against Tyre and Sidon in our last lesson, so we skip ahead now to chapter 24. The theme of this section is worldwide judgment, and it is part of a larger block of material, which includes chapters 25 through 27. This entire section has sometimes been called "The Little Apocalypse."

When we read these words, we wish the prophet had been more specific about when he expected these incidents to occur. My guess is that he was so discouraged by the moral and spiritual depravity of his day that he thought of the world in his time as being ripe for judgment. Perhaps this is why he expects a judgment similar to that which God brought upon the world in the days of Noah. Then, too, there are some interpreters who see this as a description of what will happen at the end of time as we know it when God will act in judgment of sin and evil.

Worldwide Desolation

This section opens with a picture of total devastation on a worldwide scale (24:1–3; see also Jeremiah 4:23–26). It is an awesome description of universal desolation—an empty earth, laid waste, turned upside down, people scattered.

Then follows a poignant description of the agony of earth and people that have come under God's judgment for their sinful and evil ways (24:4–13). We're reminded in these verses of God's judgment on the world in the days of Noah (see also 24:18; 26:20). Isaiah charges the people with being breakers of God's laws and of violating God's eternal covenant, probably the one with Noah that included all of the people of the earth (see Genesis 9:1–17). Under the Noah covenant all people everywhere were to follow and obey certain moral laws, including the law against murder. And because of the violation of that law, the "earth dries up and crumbles away, the mainland dries out and crumbles away, the exalted of the people of the earth dwindle" (24:4, NASB). But there's more: "The earth is also defiled by its inhabitants. . . . Therefore, a curse devours the earth, and those who live on it suffer for their guilt" (24:5–6, NASB).

The entire scene is one of intense agony, but the writer lays special emphasis on an unnamed city that is especially hard hit by the judgment (24:10–12). There has been a great deal of speculation as to the identity of this city. Some see it as Jerusalem, others as Samaria or Babylon. It is possible, though, that the prophet has given us a symbol of all great powers that oppose and defy the will of God and oppress the people of God. Most certainly, a survey of history from the days of Isaiah to the present reveals the truth that any nation that turns its back on God comes to judgment one way or another.

A Time of Premature Praise

Next we find three verses that are difficult to fit into the context of the chapter (24:14–16). Described here is a time of singing and shouting with the prophet refusing to participate. As far as he was concerned there was no reason to celebrate and offer praise as long as treacherous people still wielded power over others (24:16). Isaiah stood tall and alone against the prevailing mood of the people of Jerusalem and Judah.

Sometimes we are called upon to stand in opposition to the prevailing mood in our society. An action is not necessarily right simply because a majority of the people support it. Our need today, as it was in Isaiah's day, is for people of deep convictions who are not afraid to stand up for goodness and justice, regardless of the consequences. Furthermore, we need interpreters of the gospel of Christ, who with integrity point out the difference between what is popular and what is right in the sight of God.

Inescapable Judgment

As Isaiah continues now, he returns to the mood expressed in verses 4 through 13. Using vivid imagery, he speaks of the earth reeling and staggering under the judgment of God (24:17–20). One of the figures of speech used to describe the judgment is the opening of the windows of heaven (24:18). Once again Isaiah seems to be comparing the future judgment to what happened in the days of Noah (see Genesis 7:11). For us, the reading of these verses may seem puzzling, but the prophet's meaning is clear—no one nor any nation can violate God's will and purposes and avoid the consequences of His judgment.

Messages of Praise and Promise (24:21–27:1)

We come now to a collection of prophetic materials that looks ahead to the final righteous rule and triumph of the Lord. Here is a grand hymn of assurance and confidence in the Lord and in the promise of His rule, not only over His chosen people of Israel but over all people everywhere who are faithful in obedience to Him.

The Lord Reigns on Mount Zion

First, the prophet speaks of the Lord in a dual role; He is both righteous Judge and glorious King (24:21–23). It is true there is a continuation here of the judgment theme (see verses 3–13, 17–20), but with one important variation. Here the prophet speaks of God's judgment of "the host of heaven, in heaven" (24:21, ESV). This could refer to the sun, moon, and stars, which ancient pagan people conceived as deities, but which the people of Israel were forbidden to worship. But the reference may also include angels and other heavenly beings (see Isaiah 6:1–3) as the New American Standard Bible interprets it: "the LORD will punish the rebellious angels of heaven on high." Either way, the prophet looks to that day when all of the cosmic world and all people everywhere will be subject to God's judgment.

But then the mood shifts from judgment to triumph as the prophet focuses on that day when "moon will be dismayed, the sun ashamed; for the LORD Almighty will reign on Mount Zion and in Jerusalem" (24:23, NIV). There is a striking similarity between what is said here and the words of the writer of the book of Revelation when he speaks of the Lord's reign over the New Jerusalem: "And the city had no need of the sun, neither of the moon, to shine in it: for the glory of God did lighten it, and the Lamb is the light thereof" (21:23, KJV). This is a good example of the New Testament fulfillment of an Old Testament promise.

A Hymn of Thanksgiving

This hymn of thanksgiving (25:1–5) celebrates the destruction of a hostile alien city (25:1–2). Since no city is mentioned by name, it probably applies to every city that would oppose the Lord and oppress His people. In bringing about the destruction of the city, the Lord identifies Himself with the poor and needy among His people and becomes for them a stronghold in time of distress, a refuge from the storm, and a shade from the heat (25:4–5). The reference to the "storm" and the "heat" is symbolic of the oppression of the "poor" and "needy." Here and throughout all of our Bible we catch God's concern for those who are poor and who suffer oppression of *any* kind.

The Lord Prepares a Feast on Mount Zion

Continuing to use the picture language of poet and prophet, Isaiah now writes about the Lord preparing a banquet and inviting everyone to attend (25:6–9). This is the first of several passages in the Bible that refer to a great banquet prepared by the Lord in the "end time" (see Zechariah 14:16–21; Matthew 22:1–14; Luke 22:28–30; Revelation 19:9). This banquet concept seems to have been suggested in the annual celebration of the Feast of Tabernacles (Exodus 23:16)—a celebration of thanksgiving at harvest time comparable to our Thanksgiving. The inclusion of all people in the invitation meant that Jews and Gentiles alike would share in the riches of God's kingdom (see also 19:19–25; 56:3–8; 66:18–21; Zechariah 2:11; 8:20–23; 14:16).

Two other actions of the Lord are mentioned in connection with the great feast. First, He destroys "the covering cast over all people" (25:7, KJV). The "covering" or "veil" (NASB) symbolizes mourning or grief (see 2 Samuel 15:30; 19:4; Esther 6:12; Jeremiah 14:3–4). Here it probably refers to the agony inflicted by tyrant nations such as the dreaded Assyrians who constantly plagued the smaller nations in the Near East. Here the prophet sees relief from this oppression, and the fact that it takes place "on this mountain" means that the place of the Assyrians' defeat is at Jerusalem (see 14:24–25; 30:31–33; 37:33–37).

Second, the Lord "will swallow up death in victory," wiping away the tears from the faces of His people and taking away their reproach (25:8, KJV). There is no way, of course, that this can be regarded as having been fulfilled in Isaiah's lifetime.

The Apostle Paul saw the fulfillment of these words as having begun with the death and resurrection of our Lord and as being completed in *our* resurrection at the time of His return (see 1 Corinthians 15:25–26, 54–56; see also Revelation 21:3–4). A little later the prophet gives us one of only two Old Testament references to resurrection (Isaiah 26:19; see also Daniel 12:2), as he continues the theme of the final conquest of death. Centuries later Paul could say of the risen Christ, "For he must reign until he has put all his enemies under his feet. The last enemy to be destroyed is death" (1 Corinthians 15:25–26, ESV).

Next, Isaiah writes of the glad response of the people to God's redemptive actions on their behalf: "Surely this is our God; we trusted in him, and he saved us. This is the LORD, we trusted in him; let us rejoice and be glad in his salvation" (25:9, NIV). Here we see a mighty chorus offering praise to God for His great salvation (see also 12:1–6).

Praise is the most appropriate expression of our gratitude to God for His deliverance and care for us. The Israelites sang God's praises after they had been delivered from Pharoah's army at the Red Sea (Exodus 15:1–12). Later Isaiah calls upon the "ruins of Jerusalem" (NIV) to "[break] forth together into singing" (52:9, ESV). The occasion for this expression of praise was the destruction of Babylon and the liberation of the Jewish exiles, "for the LORD has comforted his people; he has redeemed Jerusalem" (ESV).

The faith of the New Testament is also a singing faith. The writer of the book of Revelation describes the scene in heaven when thousands upon thousands of voices will sing, "Worthy is the Lamb that was slaughtered to receive power, wealth, wisdom, might, honor, glory, and blessing. . . . To Him who sits on the throne and to the Lamb *be* the blessing, the honor, the glory, and the dominion forever and ever" (5:12–13, NASB). Praise, not doom and gloom, are the attractive marks of a Christian.

The Doom of Moab

Once again, we have an abrupt shift in mood as the writer draws a sharp contrast between the glorious events taking place on the mountain of the Lord and the horrible fate awaiting Moab (25:10–12). While the nations of the world feast at the Lord's banquet table (25:6), Moab is "trampled" like straw in "the manure" (25:10, NIV). While in this case the prophet singles out the Moabites for special attention, it is likely he was using them as a symbol of all people and nations who reject the Lord. The dreadful scene the prophet has given us here is reminiscent of the stark description of the bottomless pit described by the writer of the book of Revelation (9:1–4).

A Tale of Two Cities

Isaiah next speaks of two cities (26:1–6). The first, "a strong city" (26:1, NIV), is the recipient of the Lord's blessing. The second, "the lofty city" (26:5, NIV), is the recipient of God's anger. The favored city is to be identified as Jerusalem. Various theories have been proposed regarding the identity of the doomed city, but many would interpret it as Babylon.

These verses take the form of a hymn celebrating the great salvation of the Lord and the security of everyone who places trust in Him. The security that comes from trusting in the Lord is one of the primary themes in the preaching of Isaiah (see 7:4, 9; 8:11–13; 28:16; 30:15). Some of the greatest words of the Old Testament come together in this hymn, words like "salvation," "truth," "peace," and "trust."

The hymn describes the righteous as those who keep the truth (26:2), whose minds are stayed on the Lord (26:3), and whose trust is always in Him (26:3b, 4). The people of God are blessed by being allowed to participate in the Lord's salvation (26:1), to enter into His presence (26:2), and to receive His perfect peace (26:3). The third of these blessings, "perfect peace," appears in Hebrew as *"shalom, shalom"*—"peace, peace." The idea behind this twice-repeated word is that of well-being, security, completion, wholeness, abundance, and fulfillment.

Bible readers often have a list of their favorite verses. We come now to one that has been committed to memory by and beloved of many people of faith over the years: "You will keep in perfect peace those whose minds are steadfast, because they trust in you" (26:3, NIV).

An Urgent Plea and a Surprising Response

As the people of Israel think back on their recent history, they confess their shortcomings and plead to the Lord for deliverance from their troubles (26:7–19). In this prayer they do not ask that His judgments be suspended, for they know that it has been during their times of trial they have learned to wait on Him: "Indeed, while following the way of Your judgments, LORD, we have waited for You eagerly" (26:8, NASB) and "Learn righteousness" (26:9, NASB). Furthermore, they readily admit that it is only when the Lord's "hand is lifted up" to punish them that they see the error of their ways and are ashamed (26:11, NASB).

As they continue to reflect prayerfully, they remember that the Lord's judgments have come and gone throughout their history, as foreign rulers have been allowed to rule over them for a time and then they were destroyed (26:13–14). The people of Israel, on the other hand, have been preserved by the Lord (26:15).

Now, however, the people are sorely distressed because the Lord's chastening hand has once again been raised against them (26:16–18). This may refer to one of the many assaults the Assyrians launched against them. But this time their appeals to the Lord have gone unanswered. They have not been delivered and their oppressors have not fallen.

The frustration of unanswered prayer is nowhere better described than in these verses. It is like the pain and frustration of a pregnant woman whose time of delivery has come but who has not been able to deliver (26:17–18). To carry this description further—the people have prayed that they might experience a new birth of freedom, but their prayers have only produced false labor.

Through the words of the prophet, we now have the Lord's surprising response to their plea (26:19). Earlier we referred to this verse as being one of only two references in the Old Testament to the future resurrection of the dead. Now they are to understand that even death itself cannot defeat God's purpose, for the righteous dead would live again. This was a great leap forward in Israel's understanding of God's eternal purpose, and while they were unable to grasp the resurrection as it was revealed in Jesus Christ, they had taken an important step in that direction.

The Lord's Mighty Sword

Again, employing colorful and poetic language, the prophet pictures the Lord enraged against the insidious forces of evil (26:20–27:1). Reminiscent of His instructions to Noah at the time he entered the ark and/or His instructions to the people of Israel at the time of the first Passover in Egypt, the Lord warns His people to go into their houses and *shut their doors* until the time of the Lord's judgment is over.

Highly symbolic language is used to describe the Lord's victory over all tyrant nations (27:1). These tyrant nations are described in mythical terms as animals, much the same as in the book of Daniel (see Daniel 7:1–8, 15–27) or in the book of Revelation (see Revelation 13:1–9). One is called "Leviathan the fleeing serpent," another is referred to as "Leviathan the twisted serpent," and a third is called "the dragon that is in the sea" (ESV). It is difficult to identify the particular nations the prophet had in mind in these references, but it is likely that Egypt and Assyria would be included among them.

The Lord's Blueprint for Israel's Future (27:2–13)

This part of our scripture lesson is composed of several brief messages that provide a happy ending to chapters 24–27. These messages stand in sharp contrast to the dire predictions of judgment that precede them.

The New Vineyard Song

The second Song of the Vineyard (27:2–6) stands in sharp contrast to the first one (see 5:1–7). The lyrics of both songs describe the loving care that the Lord gave the vineyard (5:1–2; 27:2–5), and both identify the vineyard as the people of Israel (5:7; 27:6). But the similarities end here. In the first song, Israel was rebellious and produced wild grapes instead of good fruit (5:2, 7). But in the second song, Israel is obedient to the Lord and fills the whole earth with its fruit (27:6).

In the first song, the Lord announced His intention to abandon the vineyard to destruction (5:5–6); here He declares His resolve to defend it against all threats (27:3–5). Whoever dares attack the vineyard must surrender and make peace with God or else be utterly destroyed.

How can we explain the contrast between the first "Song of the Vineyard" (5:1–7) and the second (27:2–6)? It likely means that God's purpose in judging His people was not to destroy them but to purify them and to restore them to fellowship with Him. Now, as then, He is not willing that any should perish but that all should come to repentance (2 Peter 3:9).

Through Trouble to Triumph

We come now to a rather confusing part of our scripture lesson (27:7–13). The first five verses are filled with so many obscure references that it has baffled interpreters. However, it seems to describe a time of trouble through which Israel (called Jacob here in verse 9) must pass before its sin has been purged. Once the purging ended, restoration would take place. The restoration is described first in terms of the harvesting of a crop of grain. From "the flowing stream of the Euphrates to the brook of Egypt" (the Nile), the Lord threshes His sheaves, bringing them in "one by one" (27:12, NASB). When we sing the old gospel song "Bringing in the Sheaves," we are echoing the prophet's words.

In addition, the restoration is described in terms of a trumpet call, like early-morning reveille, alerting the scattered troops to assemble. The call is for the exiles now living in Assyria and Egypt to assemble on Mount Zion (Jerusalem) in order to worship the Lord (27:13). This is the first of many references in the Bible to the blowing of the trumpet to signal the beginning of God's new day (see Matthew 24:31; 1 Corinthians 15:51–52; 1 Thessalonians 4:16–17; Revelation 8:2). The blowing of the trumpet is an appropriate ending to "the Little Apocalypse," as chapters 24 through 27 have sometimes been called.

Messages for Hard Times (28:1–32:20)

Most of the messages in this section are addressed to Israel and Judah against the background of the crises they confronted during the last half of the eighth century BC. Because Assyria provoked most of these crises, this section has been labeled "The Assyrian Cycle of Prophecies."

A Society Ruled by Drunkards

This first message is addressed to the leaders of Ephraim, another name for the northern kingdom of Israel (28:1–13). This is dated before 722 BC, for this was the date of the Assyrian conquest of Israel. There was no kingdom of Israel after 722 BC; only the kingdom of Judah remained.

Isaiah's message to Israel was that its days were numbered. Time was running out for stumbling, bumbling, drunken leaders. Samaria, their lovely capital, was only a fading flower. Soon it and its drunken leaders would be trampled underfoot by one who was "mighty and strong" (28:2–4)—referring to the king of Assyria.

The drunkards of Ephraim are twice referred to as their nation's "proud crown" (28:1, NASB) and "splendid crown" (verse 3, NASB). However, unlike this crown of fading beauty (see 28:4), the Lord would be an everlasting "crown of glory" (KJV) for those who managed to survive the destruction of the land (28:4–6).

Isaiah now turned to the prophets and priests of Judah and made the same accusation against them that he had made earlier against the leaders of the northern kingdom of Israel. He accused them of allowing wine and strong drink to cloud their vision and distort their judgment (28:7).

The prophet's words hit home, and Judah's leaders struck back at him. They asked who appointed him to be their teacher, and mocked him for lecturing them about their responsibilities. They accused him of treating them like little children who knew nothing and are barely weaned (28:9–10).

Isaiah responded with an ominous prophecy of judgment against Jerusalem and its drunken leaders (28:11–13). Since they refused to learn lessons taught in their own language, the Lord would speak to them in another language, meaning of course the language of the Assyrians. The rest and peace that could have been theirs would be taken from them, and they would be hopelessly destroyed. Five different verbs (set in italic type here for identification purposes) are used at the end of verse 13 to stress the finality of their destruction—"as they *go* they will *fall* backward; they will be *injured* and *snared* and *captured*."

A Covenant with Death

The prophet next directs his attention to Jerusalem's leaders, the undisciplined "scoffers" who engineered the "covenant with death" (28:14–22, ESV). It is likely this refers to a treaty made between Hezekiah and Pharoah Shabako of Egypt, who ruled 710–696 BC. Isaiah was opposed to the treaty from the start, for he thought of Egypt as a worthless ally against the might of Assyria (see 30:1–7; 31:1–3). He felt even more strongly that for Judah to trust in any outside help was to place the power of kings and armies above the power of God. He reminded the supporters of the treaty that the Egyptians were only humans and not God, and that their horses were only flesh and not spirit (see 31:3).

Isaiah used a powerful figure of speech to describe the inadequacy of Judah's foreign policy. It was the figure of a bed too short for a man to stretch himself upon, and of a cover too narrow for him to wrap himself in (28:20). Imagine the discomfort of someone having to spend a cold night in a bed like that!

Isaiah also predicted that a powerful storm would soon sweep through the land and destroy Judah's flimsy shelter (28:17–19). This prediction was fulfilled when Sennacherib, king of Assyria, invaded Judah and laid siege to Jerusalem in 701 BC.

Isaiah's advice, however, was not all negative. He recommended the way of faith as the alternative to frustration and defeat. In every crisis he encountered, he sounded this same note (see 7:4, 9; 30:15; 32:16–18; 37:6–7). One of Isaiah's principal contributions to the religion of Israel was his stress upon the importance of faith to a right relationship with God.

The prophet's advice is contained in these memorable words, "Behold, I am laying a stone in Zion, a tested stone, a precious cornerstone for the foundation, firmly placed. The one who believes in it will not be disturbed. I will make justice the measuring line and righteousness the level" (28:16–17, NASB). As opposed to the phony security assured by Jerusalem's leaders, Isaiah speaks of an authentic security offered by God.

God was providing an alternative foundation to that which Judah had laid for itself. His foundation was dependable and sure, for it was built of stones carefully selected for their beauty and strength (28:16). The Hebrew word translated "a tested stone" occurs nowhere else in the Old Testament. One Hebrew dictionary suggests that it is an Egyptian loanword describing a quality of fine-grained stone especially suitable for the carving of inscriptions. This suggests to us that God's foundation stone also bore a message, and that the message is stated at the end of verse 16: "the one who relies on it will never be stricken with panic" (NIV). These words take us to the very heart of Isaiah's theology. He firmly believed that without a foundation of trust in the Lord there could be no personal or national security (see also 26:1–3).

The prophet continues to use building metaphors in verse 17, where he speaks of the "measuring line" and the "level" (NASB). The line is defined here as "justice," and the level as "righteousness." Measuring lines and levels were used then, as they still are today, for raising walls and for ensuring that they were straight and plumb. By using these metaphors, Isaiah was saying that a nation whose foundation is trust in God and whose walls conform to the standards of justice and righteousness will endure. These same metaphors can well apply to the conduct of our state and national governments today. Foreign policy regulated by justice and righteousness could completely reorder the agenda for the rest of the twenty-first century and beyond!

The Parable of the Farmer

Isaiah now gives us a parable (28:23–29) told in the style of the wisdom teacher (28:1; see Proverbs 1:8; 3:1; 4:1–2, 10). The purpose of the parable of the farmer answers a complaint made by the people of Judah against the Lord. They accused Him of failing to match their punishment with their crime. In other words, they contended that God had been too hard on them. The parable teaches that God is at least as knowledgeable as the experienced farmer, who fits his cultivation methods to the seasons and his harvesting methods to the crops. Isaiah believed that God's judgment was a necessary but temporary activity; His ultimate purpose is the salvation of His people.

Jerusalem's Distress and Deliverance

Isaiah's next prophecy (29:1–8) consists of two distinct parts. The first foretells a disastrous siege of Jerusalem by Sennacherib in 701 BC (29:1–4). Jerusalem is addressed as Ariel (29:1–2, 7), an unusual word that in Ezekiel 43:15–16 is rendered "altar." The point being made is that even though the city houses God's altar, it will not be saved from the coming destruction.

The second part of the passage pictures a complete change in Jerusalem's fortunes (29:5–8). Its attackers suddenly withdraw, with nothing to show for their efforts. The reference here is to the intervention of the Lord, which caused Sennacherib to withdraw his troops from the siege of Jerusalem. The prophet describes the scene: "Then the angel of the LORD went out and struck 185,000 in the camp of the Assyrians; and when the rest got up early in the morning, behold, all of the 185,000 were dead. So Sennacherib the king of Assyria departed and returned home and lived in Nineveh" (Isaiah 37:36–37, NASB).

Blindness and Hypocrisy

In these next verses (29:9–14) Isaiah describes the spiritual stupor of the people of Judah just before 701 BC. They were a blind people (29:9–12), and their only service to God was lip service (29:13–14). They were totally without spiritual insight. The description of their blindness reminds us of the words spoken to Isaiah at the time of his call (see 6:9–10).

Of particular interest in these verses is the statement that God had caused the people's blindness (29:10). This is a testimony to the strict monotheistic faith of the Old Testament writers, who regarded God as the ultimate cause of everything that happened (see Isaiah 45:7; Exodus 10:20; 1 Samuel 16:14; 2 Samuel 24:1).

The Parable of the Potter

Isaiah now gives us a short prophecy (29:15–16) that, in form, closely resembles an earlier one (10:15). Both ask how something created could dare challenge the power and authority of its Creator. The question was first directed to the arrogant Assyrians (10:15), but here it is addressed to the proud rulers of Judah who were attempting to circumvent the will of God and enter into an alliance with Egypt that would be a secret *even from God.* The prophet is accusing them of mocking God and compares them to clay pots that criticize the potter who shaped them. In their attempt to criticize and fool God, they were not only foolishly arrogant but also guilty of attitudes that could best be described as practical atheism.

Transformation in the New Age

Amid everything that is discouraging, Isaiah, the prophet of hope, next looks into the future and sees a spiritual transformation of God's people (29:17–24). It would be a time when their deafness would be replaced by hearing, and blindness by new sight (29:18; see also verses 10–12), and when the meek and the poor of the earth would find new joy in the Lord (29:19).

The prophet saw this new golden age for his people as a time of peace and reconciliation and restoration—a time when they would be free from the harassment of their enemies (29:20–24). As in other related prophecies, we have no indication as to when the prophet expected these dreams to be fulfilled.

The Folly of Trusting in Egypt

In this next part of our scripture lesson (30:1–17), Isaiah gives four brief messages of doom (verses 1–5; 6–7; 8–14; and 15–17). They all belong to the troubled period leading up to Sennacherib's invasion of Judah in 701 BC (see 28:14–22).

At this point in history Egypt was ruled by a very able pharoah named Shabako (710–696 BC). Hezekiah, faced with the threat of invasion from Assyria, had sent representatives to Egypt to seek Shabako's help.

Isaiah had opposed this plan for two reasons. The first was that the men of Judah had acted on their own authority without consulting the Lord or seeking His counsel (30:1–2). The second reason was that Isaiah considered Egypt to be unreliable and its help worthless (30:3–5).

The prophet next described the difficult journey that Hezekiah's representatives had to make across the Sinai desert on their way to Egypt. It was a harsh and forbidding land, and leading a caravan of asses and camels loaded with rich gifts for the Egyptians was a strenuous task (30:6). Furthermore, Isaiah saw it as a futile trip because the Egyptians promised much but delivered little (30:7).

There is bitter irony in the fact that the people of Judah would send to Egypt for help, because centuries before, it was the Egyptians who had oppressed and enslaved them. It is also ironic that the camel caravan bearing expensive gifts to buy Egypt's favor had to make the dangerous journey across the miles of barren desert separating Judah from Egypt. The Sinai desert is one of the most inhospitable regions on the earth. Is it any wonder that Isaiah ridiculed the leaders who sent them on this useless mission?

Because the people of Judah stubbornly refused to listen to Isaiah's preaching, the third prophecy in this series opens with the prophet being told to put his message into writing. This gave it something of the form of a legal paper that could serve at some future date as a witness (30:8). The language of the message is strong: they are "a rebellious people, lying children, children that will not hear the law of the LORD" (30:9, KJV). In addition, the people of Judah insisted that their seers and prophets not confront them with the truth. Instead, they wanted only to hear what would make them feel good even though it might not be the truth (30:10).

Isaiah, though, refused to remain silent. So, speaking on behalf of God, he pronounced judgment against the people of Judah and employed two remarkable similes to describe their fate (30:12–14). First, he compared them to a wall that suddenly gives way and crumbles. Second, he compared them to a clay pot that is shattered and useless. These vivid word pictures describe the finality of God's judgment.

Then follows one of the best-known and best-loved verses in the book of Isaiah. It repeats one of the primary themes in the prophet's preaching: "This is what the Sovereign LORD, the Holy One of Israel, says: 'In repentance and rest is your salvation, in quietness and trust is your strength, but you would have none of it'" (30:15, NIV).

Isaiah's words sounded too idealistic to the hard-nosed, practical-minded politicians of Judah. They felt more secure trusting in horses than in the promises of some wild-eyed prophet (30:16). But their fate, the prophet reminded them, would be to flee in disarray before their enemies, until only a small group of them remained (30:17; see 1:8–9; 6:9–12; 36:1). The "remnant" (1:9, KJV) likely refers to Jerusalem, the only city in Judah to escape destruction by the Assyrians in 701 BC.

A Promise of Restoration

Having predicted doom and destruction because of disobedience, the prophet now foresees future restoration (30:18–26). Through the graciousness of the Lord, the prophet sees that time when their weeping will be over and their affliction will be lifted. It is then the Lord will guide them, saying, "'This is the way, walk in it,' when you turn to the right or when you turn to the left" (30:21, ESV). It is then they would cast aside the idols they had looked to in the past for guidance (30:22).

The change in attitude on the part of the people would be accompanied by a change in nature. Ample rains will provide bread for the people (30:23), pasture for the cattle (30:24), and copious streams to water the land (30:25). And even the light from the sun and moon will seem brighter and more intense (30:26). This will be a grand time of restoration and healing.

God's Judgment of Assyria

Next, the mood of Isaiah's prophecy shifts dramatically. From the reassuring words of healing for Jerusalem and Judah, the prophet turns now and lashes out at Assyria, utilizing picture language that sends chills along our spine (30:27–33). This hated enemy of Israel and Judah and conqueror of ancient Near Eastern nations was now to be on the receiving end of God's justice as the prophet saw it. For too long the Assyrian armies had gotten away with murder and the vilest forms of cruelty. Now their day of judgment was fast approaching. Though from the comfort of our modern life, the intensity of Isaiah's predictions may cause us to shudder, it is important that we not let this stand in the way of our getting a message for our time.

It may seem at times that disruptive and evil forces are in charge of all that is going on. We may feel that wrong is on the throne and that which is good is passed by entirely. It may seem to us that evil people and insidious forces are calling the shots on a national and international scale. But a review of history from the beginning of time underlines the basic truth that sooner or later we all confront the consequences of our actions. In the final analysis, the Assyrians of every century have had to deal with both the mercy and the justice of God whom we worship and follow.

True and False Security

Once again Isaiah directs his attention to the movement of Judah's leaders to be in alliance with Egypt as a means of defense against Assyria (31:1–9). He was convinced that any dependency on Egypt spelled doom. The only answer for Judah's security was "the Holy One of Israel." On the other hand, to place their confidence in Egypt's brute force was an invitation to disaster (31:1–3).

The tone of this message changes as the prophet describes the Lord's protection of Judah in the face of the Assyrian threat (31:4–9). In colorful and descriptive language that would have been immediately understandable to his first readers and listeners, Isaiah pictures the Lord holding Jerusalem firmly in His grasp like a lion would protectively clutch his prey and as birds would hover over their young (31:4–5). With that picture firmly in mind, the Lord then invites prodigal Judah to return to Him while at the same time reminding them that true repentance involves turning away from all false gods (31:6–7).

As this prophecy draws to its conclusion, the prediction of Assyria's defeat is repeated (31:8–9). The prophet's words leave nothing to question: "And the Assyrian will fall by a sword not wielded by a man, and a sword not of man will devour him. So he will not escape the sword, and his young men will become forced laborers. 'His rock will pass away because of panic, and his officers will be terrified by the flag,' declares the LORD, whose fire is in Zion and whose furnace is in Jerusalem" (31:8–9, NASB). Again, with the use of picture language we have an apparent reference to the plague of death that forced the Assyrian army to abandon the Jerusalem siege in 701 BC (see 37:21–38). Here, too, the Lord is pictured as a fire driving back the Assyrians with its heat.

A Reign of Righteousness and Peace

With penetrating insight Isaiah now somehow looks into the future and foresees a time when Judah would be ruled by leaders devoted to righteousness and justice (32:1–5). These words are a marvelous tribute to good government. We have here a description of what life would be like in a nation governed by righteous leaders. In such a society, scoundrels and fools would be recognized for what they are, instead of pillars of the community.

Apparently, the situation in Isaiah's time was not all that different from what we experience today, when by hook or by crook people achieve leadership positions and then play the part of a fool (verse 5), misusing our trust in them. Then in verses 6 through 8 he sets out to help us see the difference between a "good-for-nothing" (AMP) fool and a wise and worthwhile person. The prophet especially emphasizes that a scoundrel or a fool is a person guilty of mistreating the poor and the needy by depriving them not only of food and drink but also of justice.

Our modern-day equivalent of what Isaiah was condemning is the stockbroker or financial management person who takes advantage of a client, a person who falsifies the conditions of a sale, the people who fudge on their income tax and rob the government of what it is rightfully due, the merchant who fails to give value for money paid, the scammers and spammers who prey upon the insecurities of unsuspecting victims via the internet or texts, the self-righteous twenty-first-century pharisees who either do nothing for the poor and hungry in their community and across the world or, worse, take advantage of the underprivileged to line their own pockets.

On the other hand, the prophet labeled as a wise person someone who gives liberally of both money and time to help those in need and is honest and upright in dealing with others. The truly wise person contributes in every way possible to those things that benefit others. The scoundrel or fool "looks out for number *one*," while the wise person truly loves a neighbor *as oneself.*

The final two prophecies in this lesson are quite different in tone. First, in chapter 32, verses 9 through 14, Isaiah has some rather harsh words for the women of Jerusalem who are "complacent" and "feel secure" (verse 9, NIV). Some Bible teachers suggest that this unusual gender-specific prophecy was directed toward women in positions of affluence and influence who lived lives of self-indulgence and had been lulled into a spirit of complacency despite warnings of danger.

The final prophecy, though, comes through in an altogether different mood (32:15–20). Pictured here is a time when God will pour out His Spirit upon His people. The earth will be restored; justice and righteousness will dictate the way of life. Everyone will live in an atmosphere of peace and tranquility. Once again, Isaiah, the prophet of hope, looks to that day when people honor the Lord and are obedient to His will.

Isaiah's God was eager to bless His people. He wanted only good for the people of Israel—and He wants only good for people in our world. With Isaiah and the writer of the book of Revelation, we, too, are called to live righteous and obedient lives now. But we also look into the future with hope to that "new heaven and a new earth"—that time when "God shall wipe away all tears" and "there shall be no more death, neither sorrow, nor crying, neither shall there be any more pain" (Revelation 21:1–4, KJV).

Savior, thank You for Your generous blessings. Your loving, overflowing nature wants to bless me more and more! Amen.

You turn things upside down, as if the potter were thought to be like the clay! Shall what is formed say to the one who formed it, "You did not make me"? Can the pot say to the potter, "You know nothing"?

—Isaiah 29:16 (NIV)

While visiting a small zoo, I became fascinated with the two-toed sloths. Though known for being slow, one of the sloths moved steadily along ropes strung from one side of his long cage to the other. He certainly wouldn't win any races, but he moved faster than I had imagined. His long, curved claws helped him maintain his grip as he gently swung upside down on his journey.

A zookeeper later pointed out that the sloths' fur grows backward from the way most animal fur does, allowing rain to flow off as they hang from tree branches. Their internal organs are also arranged to accommodate this upside-down life.

As the keeper talked, she fed the sloths bits of cucumber and zucchini, some of their favorite treats. In the wild, they eat relatively little food because it can take up to a month to digest just one leaf. The only time they drop to the ground is to defecate—once a week. Since moving on the ground exposes sloths to predators and puts undue stress on their lungs, the more they remain in the trees, the better.

Though I enjoyed hearing about the sloths, I prefer to stay right side up with my feet planted firmly on the ground. Without Jesus, though, my world would turn upside down. As my Lord and Savior, He not only keeps me right side up but also helps me stay grounded in God's Word. He is the only one who can keep me on the right path in this topsy-turvy world.

—*Tracy Crump*

Notes

Notes

LESSON 4: ISAIAH 33:1–39:8

Israel and the Nations

Savior, Your all-encompassing grace overwhelms me. I am overcome by Your relentless love. AMEN.

Note: Chapter 33 is included here simply for convenience of handling. As far as subject matter is concerned, it belongs with chapters 28–32. It is the concluding chapter in the so-called Assyrian Cycle of Prophecies.

God of Grace and Glory (33:1–24)

This part of our lesson pulls together a number of disjointed themes treated earlier in the book of Isaiah. These include the afflicting of the Lord's people by foreign oppressors (33:8–9; see 1:7–8; 5:26–30), the Lord's promise of deliverance (33:1, 10–12; see 10:24–27; 29:5–8), and the prophet's dream for a better future (33:17–24; see 2:2–4; 4:2–6; 9:1–7; 11:1–9; 25:6–9; 29:18–24).

The Denunciation of Assyria

This is the fifth time in chapters 28–33 that a prophetic message begins with the word "Woe" (see 28:1; 29:1; 29:15; 30:1). A message introduced by this word is always condemnatory in nature. Here judgment is passed upon Assyria, a nation that had achieved fame as a conqueror and destroyer of other nations (33:1). The countries conquered by the Assyrians after the middle of the eighth century BC included Babylon, Egypt, Syria, Israel, and Philistia. As Assyria had dealt treacherously with these nations, so they would now deal treacherously with Assyria. The law of the harvest applies to nations as well as to individuals—as they have sown, so shall they reap.

A Plea for Divine Help

Following the fierce denunciation of Assyria, Isaiah, in Israel's behalf, prays for divine help (33:2–4). The people express not only their commitment to wait on the Lord but also their confidence in His power to save. In verses 3 and 4 the prophet foresees divine intervention as he speaks of "tumultuous noise" (verse 3, ESV)—also note especially Isaiah 37:36–37.

A Reassuring Response

In response to their prayer, the prophet insists that it is the Lord's purpose to establish Zion (Jerusalem) as a city of "justice and righteousness" (33:5, NASB; see also 1:24–26; 32:16–17). In addition, there is the promise of national stability, rooted in wisdom, knowledge, and the fear of the Lord (33:6). These are the same qualities the writer assigned earlier to the Messianic King (11:1–2); consequently, the reference here may be to that time when the long-anticipated Messiah comes.

A Lament over a Distressed Land

Next the prophet returns to a description of the distressful situation facing Isaiah and the people of Judah near the end of the eighth century BC (33:7–9). Jerusalem's ambassadors, perhaps the same ones who sought help from Egypt (see 30:1–5), weep bitter tears of disappointment (33:7). They had counted on Egypt to help them, only to discover that Egypt's help was useless, and at the same time Jerusalem finds itself cut off from the rest of the world by the destruction of its road system (33:8).

An unnamed foe, apparently to be interpreted as the king of Assyria, had broken his covenant with them, ruthlessly attacked the cities of Israel, and killed its citizens without regard to the rights of any of them (33:8). According to the prophet, the utter desolation of the land can be seen by surveying its once rich farming districts, districts like Lebanon, Sharon, Bashan, and Carmel (33:9). Lebanon and Carmel were part of the mountain range in the central part of Palestine; Sharon was the fertile coastal plain stretching along the Mediterranean; and Bashan was the fertile pastureland east of the Jordan River. These had been taken out of production, and the whole land mourned and languished.

God's Promise of Salvation

In response to Israel's lament over the desolation of its land, the Lord now pronounces judgment on those who have dared oppress His people (33:10). The meaning of verse 11 is that the oppressors' policies are self-destructive. People and nations that live by the sword shall also die by the sword. The Apostle Paul put it this way: "Whatever a person sows, this he will also reap" (Galatians 6:7, NASB). The enemy's defeat is pictured here as a massive inferno brought on by their own crimes against humanity (33:11–12). Prophecies like this must have given the hard-pressed Israelites great hope.

Requirements for Participation in God's Kingdom

As Isaiah continues to look ahead to that crucial time of coming judgment, he addresses himself to both "you who are far away"—the Gentiles—and "you who are near"—those Israelites that are disobedient (33:13–16, NIV). And he asks in effect, "What does God require for us to make our lives truly pleasing to Him?" This was a question that was raised over and over again in Old Testament times. These are some of the other forms this same question takes (quoted from the New International Version of the Bible):

- "LORD, who may dwell in your sacred tent? Who may live on your holy mountain?" (Psalm 15:1).
- "Who may ascend the mountain of the LORD? Who may stand in his holy place?" (Psalm 24:3).
- "With what shall I come before the LORD and bow down before the exalted God? Shall I come before him with burnt offerings, with calves a year old? Will the LORD be pleased with thousands of rams, with ten thousand rivers of olive oil? Shall I offer my firstborn for my transgression, the fruit of my body for the sin of my soul?" (Micah 6:6–7).

The Lord always takes questions like these very seriously, and in each of the verses cited here He spells out His requirements in clear terms. It is worth noting that He is concerned not only with how we relate to Him but also about how we relate to our fellow human beings. It is impossible to be rightly related to God unless we are also rightly related to one another.

(Take a moment to read the verses immediately following those we quoted above: Psalms 15:2–5; 24:4; Micah 6:8.)

Once Isaiah had described the fiery judgment awaiting cruel and tyrant nations like Assyria (33:11–12), some of the Israelites became concerned about their own safety. They were not sure they were prepared to meet God if He should loose His judgment upon the world. They cried out in dread, "Who among us can live with the consuming fire? Who among us can live with everlasting burning?" (33:14, NASB).

This was a common reaction for persons who thought about having to meet God face-to-face. Perhaps you recall how Isaiah himself responded when he saw a vision of the Lord sitting upon His heavenly throne and heard the seraphim singing of His holiness. Isaiah cried out in alarm: "Woe is me! For I am lost; for I am a man of unclean lips, and I dwell in the midst of a people of unclean lips; for my eyes have seen the King, the Lord of hosts!" (6:5, ESV). Looking only at ourselves may leave us self-satisfied, but looking at the Lord reminds us of how far short we fall from living our lives in accordance with His will.

Isaiah next spells out the Lord's requirements for those who would share in His kingdom and live in His presence (33:15). The practical nature of these requirements is striking: "Those who walk righteously and speak what is right, who reject gain from extortion and keep their hands from accepting bribes, who stop their ears against plots of murder and shut their eyes against contemplating evil" (NIV).

Each of the requirements in this "code of conduct" involves a separate bodily action: walking, speaking, refusing, shaking out one's hands, stopping one's ears, and closing one's eyes. The first two requirements outline what the righteous person *should* do. The rest indicate what the righteous person should *not* do. The requirements are that they walk and talk and act in a manner worthy of persons in a right relationship with God; and that they *not* enrich themselves by exploiting the poor; that they *not* accept bribes; that they *not* become involved in bloodshed, evidently referring to murder; and that they *not* look upon the "evil" or misfortunes of others.

Not a single one of these requirements involves what we might think of today as "church" responsibilities. They are related instead to our duties toward other human beings. We're told here that we should protect the rights of others if we expect the Lord to protect us. It may well be that we are unprepared to live with the Lord unless we have first learned how to live with one another. The New Testament writer put it more strongly: "Whoever claims to love God yet hates a brother or sister is a liar. For whoever does not love their brother and sister, whom they have seen, cannot love God, whom they have not seen. And he has given us this command: Anyone who loves God must also love their brother and sister" (1 John 4:20–21, NIV).

This section closes with a promise of well-being to the person who satisfies God's requirements: "They are the ones who will dwell on the heights, whose refuge will be the mountain fortress. Their bread will be supplied, and water will not fail them" (33:16, NIV; see Psalms 15:5; 24:5). It would be difficult to find a better description of personal security than this.

The King in His Beauty

Now the prophet describes the glorious future he saw awaiting God's people during the future reign of Messiah (33:17–24). The key verbs in these verses are "see," "look," and "behold" (33:17, 19–20). Drawing on poetic picture-language, Isaiah describes the beginning of the Messiah's reign as a time when people would rub their eyes in amazement at the glory that surrounded them. They would see the Messianic King in all His beauty and a prosperous land that stretched far into the distance (33:17), and they would see Jerusalem—New Jerusalem—established as a place where God lived and ruled.

Any threat of invasion was now a thing of the past, for the Lord God was their Judge, their Lawgiver, their King, and their Savior (33:22). The prophet rounded out the picture of the glorious future of the Lord's people with a promise that their diseases would be healed and their sins forgiven (33:24). The promise of forgiveness furnished an appropriate conclusion to this prophecy, for it is the greatest promise of all.

Judah's Source of Security

Chapter 33 is the concluding part of the so-called Assyrian Cycle of Prophecies, prophecies related to the crisis of 701 BC, when the Assyrians besieged Jerusalem (see 36:1–37:38). Throughout this crisis Isaiah hammered home his message that Judah's only security lay in trusting the Lord (see 28:16; 29:1–3, 15, 18; 31:8; 32:17; 33:20–22). The adequacy of divine power is nowhere more clearly stated than here.

A Phony Security

There are two points that we need to emphasize in the study of this part of Isaiah. The first is that it is a sign of arrogance and unbelief for God's people to turn away from Him and place their trust in military might. The Psalmist underlined this point when he wrote, "The king is not saved by his great army; a warrior is not delivered by his great strength. The war horse is a false hope for salvation, and by its great might it cannot rescue. Behold, the eye of the LORD is on those who fear him, on those who hope in his steadfast love, that he may deliver their soul from death and keep them alive in famine" (Psalm 33:16–19, ESV).

If we substitute the mighty weapons produced by scientists and engineers in our day for the war horse mentioned in the psalm, the message is still true. Jesus said that "all who draw the sword will die by the sword " (Matthew 26:52, NIV). His words have stood the test of more than two thousand years of history.

It is easy, when we are confident in our armed forces and our stockpile of weapons and technology, to believe that our true strength and security lie in these alone. Politicians might even have their own selfish reasons for encouraging us to believe this. They are often not so much concerned with strengthening the defenses of the country as they are with feathering their own nests or gaining more political power. The end of the Cold War brought about a welcome reduction of nuclear stockpiles in the two superpowers of that day, but with other nations advancing and pursuing their own nuclear programs, we must realize anew that, ultimately, it is God in whom we must place our trust for peace and protection—not human leaders or institutions.

The Source of Life's Richest Rewards

The second point to take away from the study of these chapters is that faith in God plus faithful service to Him leads to joy, peace, and fullness of life. In other words, life's richest rewards are given to those who learn how to "trust and obey."

In the crisis of 701 BC, when the Assyrian armies encircled the city of Jerusalem and threatened its destruction, Isaiah's recommendation of trust in God must have sounded too naive and idealistic to the hard-nosed politicians. What did the prophet mean by affirming that Judah's true strength lay in trusting God and practicing justice rather than in forming foreign alliances and strengthening its defenses? They thought he wanted them to embrace an impossible dream.

Isaiah's advice is still valid today, and it is reflected in the words of the Psalmist: "Be still and know (recognize, understand) that I am God. I will be exalted among the nations! I will be exalted in the earth" (Psalm 46:10, AMP).

Judgment against the Nations (34:1–17)

Chapters 34–35 of the book of Isaiah are generally regarded as coming from the same time period as chapters 40–66—the exilic or early post-exilic period (587–537 BC). This view is based on the fact that the two sections are so alike in style, vocabulary, and theological perspective. They probably became separated from each other when the historical materials in chapters 36–39, largely borrowed from 2 Kings 18:13–20:19, were included in the book.

Actually, chapters 34 and 35 belong together. Chapter 34 speaks of the downfall of the nations of the world, and chapter 35 speaks of the restoration of Zion (Jerusalem).

The Lord's Anger against Foreign Nations

We come now to a vivid description of worldwide judgment (34:1–4). The language used here is full of metaphors that sound strange to our ears. It is the prophet's way of saying that God will not let the nations of the world off the hook until all their sins are judged. Isaiah gives us no clue as to why the Lord's anger is unleashed against the world powers. We're simply told in no uncertain terms that their doom is sealed (34:1–3).

In addition, utilizing colorful imagery, Isaiah sees the Lord's judgment affecting the entire universe. "All the stars in the sky will be dissolved and the heavens rolled up like a scroll; all the starry host will fall like withered leaves from the vine, like shriveled figs from the fig tree" (34:4, NIV). The same imagery is used to describe the great judgment in Revelation 6:13–14.

The Doom of Edom

Next to Babylon, Edom was the nation most hated by the Jews (34:5–17). The animosity between these two nations had a long history. The Bible says it began when their respective ancestors, Jacob and Esau, struggled together in the womb of their mother, Rebekah (Genesis 25:21–23). It was aggravated further by Jacob's use of questionable means to acquire his brother's birthright (see Genesis 25:29–34) and his blessing (see Genesis 27:1–41).

The feud between the Edomites, descendants of Esau, and the Israelites, descendants of Jacob, continued throughout the whole panorama of biblical history (see Numbers 20:14–21). But the Edomites dealt their cruelest blow to the Israelites when they assisted the Babylonians in the destruction of Jerusalem in 587 BC (see Obadiah 10–14; Psalm 137:7). After this "stab in the back," it was easy for the Israelites to believe that the Lord Himself must hate the Edomites (see Isaiah 63:1–6; Jeremiah 49:17–22; Ezekiel 25:12–14; 35:1–15; Malachi 1:2–5). An interesting footnote was added to this history when the Romans appointed Herod the Great, an Edomite, to rule over the province of Judea in the days of Jesus (see Luke 1:5).

The judgment of Edom is described here by Isaiah as a sacrifice that the Lord would perform at Bozrah, the capital of the country (34:5–8). Idumea, mentioned in verses 5 and 6, refers to the territory west of the Dead Sea that the Edomites occupied soon after the destruction of Jerusalem in 587 BC. At the great sacrifice being prepared by the Lord, the Edomites and all their cattle would be slain (34:5–7). This was seen as the time of the Lord's vengeance against Edom for the treachery against His people.

The imagery of the judgment against Edom changes in verses 9 and 10 from that of a sword and a sacrifice to brimstone and burning pitch. This reminds us of the story of the overthrow of

Sodom and Gomorrah (see Genesis 19:24–25), cities that, like Edom, had become proverbial for their wickedness.

Next, the prophet sees Edom reduced to a wasteland inhabited by wild beasts of the desert and demon-like creatures (34:11–15). In other words, Edom would become a desolate and haunted land, one where travelers dared not set foot.

The prophet then seems to indicate that the calamities that would befall Edom were in fulfillment of what had been written in "the book of the LORD" (34:16, ESV), and he encourages his readers to consult the book of the Lord and read it. We have no clue as to the identity of this book, but it has been variously identified as Isaiah 13–23, the entire book of Isaiah, or to pronouncements against Edom found in other prophetic writings (Amos 1:11–12; Jeremiah 49:7–22; Ezekiel 35). It also has been suggested that it might have referred to a treaty between Judah and Edom, a copy of which would have been available to any who wished to read it.

We're further told here (34:16) that all the pronouncements against Edom would be fulfilled and that the Lord Himself would divide the territory and allot portions of it to the birds, the beasts, and the demons (34:17). The prophet's threat against Edom was fulfilled sometime between 500 and 300 BC, when the country was completely taken over by a desert tribe, possibly the Nabataeans.

The Lord's Redemption of His People (35:1–10)

This part of our lesson contains some of the most comforting and encouraging words in the book of Isaiah. This collection of salvation prophecies is addressed to the Jewish exiles in Babylon who were taken captive in 587 BC. The Lord promised that He would set them free from their captors and prepare a path across the desert so that they might return in triumph to Jerusalem and Judah.

The themes introduced in chapter 35 are treated in greater detail in chapters 40–66. Some of the more prominent are these:

1. The transformation of the desert into a garden of delight (35:1–2, 6–7; see also 41:17–20; 43:19–21; 51:3; 55:12–13)
2. The proclamation of the coming of God to comfort and strengthen His people (35:3–4; see also 40:9–11; 42:13–16; 43:1–2)
3. The preparation of a highway for the returning people (35:8–9; see also 40:3–5; 49:8–12; 57:14; 62:10–12)
4. The joy of the people as they return to Jerusalem (35:10; see also 42:10–12; 44:23; 48:20, 49:13; 51:11; 52:7–10)

The Desert Shall Rejoice

The desert described in our scripture lesson is the one that lay between the Mesopotamian Valley in the north and east and the land of Judah to the south and west (35:1–2, 6–7). With poetic language, the Judean exiles are promised that when they returned from Babylon, this vast desert would be transformed into a garden of flowers and trees and streams. And to give further color and identification to the picture, the desert is said to share the glory of Lebanon, the excellency of Carmel, and the beauty of the plains of Sharon that stretch out along the Mediterranean Sea. These were regions of Palestine well-known for luxuriant growth.

Then, too, copious springs of water would completely transform the desert (35:6–7). Whereas it had once been a refuge for jackals (35:7; note that this word is incorrectly translated "dragons" in the King James Version), it would now become a place where cattle could graze and rest among the reeds and rushes.

In addition, the writer says that "the burning sand (mirage) will become a pool [of water]" (35:7, AMP), referring to the phenomenon known as a mirage, the optical illusion one often gets when traveling in the desert that looks like a large body of water in the distance. Actually, the prophet is saying that what was formerly only a mirage would now become a real lake—illusions would disappear and false hopes would become reality.

Now, the Isaiah writer at this point did not mean to say that the broad desert separating Babylon from Jerusalem would literally be changed into a well-watered garden. There is every indication that when the liberated exiles crossed the desert on their homeward journey, it remained as barren and dangerous as it had ever been (see Ezra 1:2–5; 7:6–9; 8:21–23, 31–32).

What then did the prophet mean when he spoke of the exiles' marvelous passage across the desert, a theme he returns to again and again in the succeeding chapters? Part of the answer lies in our realizing that the desert was not simply a barren waste separating the Jewish exiles from their homeland, although it was certainly this. In a larger sense, however, it was a symbol of life apart from God. The withdrawal of God from His people, symbolized by the exile, meant stagnation and death. However, the return of God, a dominant theme in this part of Isaiah, meant new vitality and new life.

Even though the desert represented danger and hardship, the Lord promised to be with the returning exiles. While the obstacles would not be removed from their pathway, He would give them the grace and strength to overcome them. This is most clearly stated in the marvelous words of the prophet when he writes: "When you pass through the waters, I will be with you; and through the rivers, they shall not overwhelm you; when you walk through fire you shall not be burned, and the flame shall not consume you" (Isaiah 43:2, ESV).

In igniting the anticipation of the trip back to Jerusalem from their exile in Babylon, the prophet pictures the desert coming alive with luxuriant growth (35:1–2). These words bring deep meaning to us today as we struggle to make sense out of our lives. Do you sometimes feel that you are stranded in some desert in your life? It is something many people experience at various times in their lives. But the thing that helps us to make our way out of the desert and continue on toward the "promised land" is the assurance that God is beside us. The Psalmist expressed this assurance in unforgettable words: "Yea, though I walk through the valley of the shadow of death, I will fear no evil: for thou art with me" (Psalm 23:4, KJV). God is ever eager to transform our deserts into gardens.

Comforting with a Word

As the prophet continues his salvation prophecies, he assumes the role of a pastor when he hears God's call to strengthen the weak hands and make firm the feeble knees (35:3). And he was told to say to those of a fearful heart, "Be strong, do not fear; your God will come, he will come with vengeance; with divine retribution he will come to save you" (35:4, NIV).

The comfort offered to the disheartened exiles far from home was not that of a cheap grace that glossed over past sins. The word of comfort was at the same time a word of judgment and a call to repentance. For too long the people of Israel had closed their eyes and refused to hear the word of the Lord (see 6:10; 29:9–12; 43:8). The prophet makes it clear that there could be no word of comfort for them unless they were willing to have their eyes opened and their ears unstopped. God's word of comfort, therefore, was both a promise for His people to believe and a command for them to obey. He would heal their blindness and deafness, provided they were willing to look and to listen (35:5; see 29:18; 30:20–21; 32:3). These words emphasize the costly and demanding character of the comfort offered by God.

The Highway of the Redeemed

Continuing the prophetic imagery related to the exiles' return to Jerusalem and Judah, the Isaiah writer speaks of a highway that was to be prepared for all who were returning (35:8–10; see also 40:3–5; 43:19; 49:8–12; 57:14; 62:10–12). This refers to the exiles who had been scattered throughout all the earth.

Three statements are made about the highway. The first is that access to it was restricted. It is called "The Way of Holiness," and for this reason unclean persons and fools would not be allowed to travel on it (35:8). The word used for fools is the same one used by the wisdom writer in Proverbs 1:7: "The fear of the Lord is the beginning of knowledge: but fools despise wisdom and instruction" (KJV). (See also Proverbs

12:15; 14:9.) It describes a hardened sinner committed to a life of folly and incapable of changing his or her ways. The word for unclean used in verse 8 is the same one Isaiah used in his great confession, "Woe is me! For I am lost; for I am a man of unclean lips, and I dwell in the midst of a people of unclean lips; for my eyes have seen the King, the LORD of hosts!" (6:5, ESV). To be unclean was to be morally defiled and thus unfit to stand in God's presence or to worship at His altar.

The second statement made about the highway is that it was a safe way. All who walked on it would be protected from beasts of prey (35:9). The idea being expressed was not clear on whether the prophet intended to say that the wild beasts would be eradicated altogether or that they would lose their ferocious nature (as is described in 11:6–9), or simply that "they will not be found there" (Isaiah 35:9, NASB). In any event, their absence from the route of returning exiles symbolized the end of violence and the dawning of the age of peace.

The third thing said about the highway across the desert is that its travelers would find everlasting joy and peace as they returned to Jerusalem. Verse 10 expresses the elemental longing of every person to arrive at the place where joy and gladness abound and where sorrow and sighing are banished forever.

A Historical Appendix (36:1–39:8)

This section of the book of Isaiah consists almost entirely of material borrowed from 2 Kings 18:13–20:19. It was apparently placed here to round out the history of Isaiah's relations with King Hezekiah, especially with regard to the events surrounding the crisis of 701 BC, when Sennacherib, king of Assyria, laid siege to Jerusalem and demanded its surrender. Isaiah counseled Hezekiah not to give in to this demand but to trust the Lord for deliverance. The prophet was vindicated when Sennacherib's invading army was wiped out by a sudden plague and the siege of the city was lifted.

The interesting thing about the events recorded here is that they have been verified by relatively recent archaeological discoveries. On reliefs from Sennacherib's palace in Nineveh, his army is pictured besieging the Judean fortress-city of Lachish, located to the southwest of Jerusalem near the Egyptian border. Sennacherib himself is portrayed as sitting upon his throne and receiving obeisance from the leaders of Lachish. The reliefs state that he laid siege to forty-six Judean walled cities and fortresses, not counting "countless small villages," and took 200,150 prisoners of war, representing most of the population of Judah at that time.

Jerusalem Besieged

Just prior to 701 BC, Hezekiah unwisely decided to revolt against Assyria. In preparation for doing so he negotiated a treaty with Egypt, one that Isaiah denounced as "a covenant with death" (28:15, NASB). Anticipating a retaliatory strike from Assyria, Hezekiah also took steps to strengthen the defenses of Jerusalem. These included having a tunnel cut through 1,700 feet of rock in order to channel the waters of the Gihon Spring into the upper pool of Siloam inside the city walls (see 2 Kings 20:20; 2 Chronicles 32:3–4). Today the curious traveler can take a guided tour through Hezekiah's tunnel.

However, Sennacherib lost no time in reasserting his authority over Hezekiah and Judah. He marched down from his capital at Nineveh, and one of his battalions followed the coastal road until it met and defeated the Egyptians at Eltekeh in the Judean foothills. Another army swept across Samaria and approached Jerusalem from the north. This battalion was led by one of Sennacherib's soldiers who bore the title of Rabshakeh, which means "chief officer." Chapter 36 describes this officer's efforts to negotiate the surrender of Jerusalem.

Rabshakeh tried to use what might be called psychological warfare against Hezekiah and his beleaguered troops. Flanked by his numerically superior forces, he stood outside the city at the very spot where Isaiah had encountered Ahaz some thirty years earlier (36:2; see 7:3). A negotiating committee chosen by Hezekiah went out to meet Rabshakeh (36:3).

Rabshakeh's speech to the committee showed his skill in the use of diplomacy. He set out to weaken the morale of the people and to undermine the authority of the king. He taunted Hezekiah—in a voice loud enough for everyone to hear—for relying on help from the king of Egypt, whom he likened to a broken reed that would pierce the hand of anyone who leaned on it for support (36:6, 9). He also chided the representatives of the people of Jerusalem for supposing that the Lord would deliver them from the king of Assyria (36:7, 10, 18–20).

When the representatives of Jerusalem asked Rabshakeh to speak in Aramaic, the diplomatic language of the day, he refused to do so, choosing instead to speak in Hebrew, so that the Jews gathered on the wall above would overhear him (36:11–12). This was a clever effort to undermine their morale and was a direct appeal to the people not to follow the counsel of Hezekiah, lest they be misled (36:13–15, 18–20).

Rabshakeh also tried to entice the people of Jerusalem to surrender, promising that those who did so would receive lenient treatment and would be taken to live in a good land, one not unlike their own (36:16–17). Like tyrants of all times, he failed to realize that the loss people fear most is the loss of their freedom.

Fortunately, the rank and file in Jerusalem were wise enough and disciplined enough to remain silent (36:21). In the meantime, the Jerusalem negotiating team returned to Hezekiah with their clothes rent in recognition of the gravity of their situation (36:22).

Jerusalem Delivered

When Hezekiah received the report of his representatives, he removed his kingly robes, dressed himself in sackcloth, and went to the Temple to pray (37:1). He also sent some of the leaders who had conferred with Rabshakeh to Isaiah the prophet to implore him to intercede on behalf of the city (37:2).

The delegation sent to Isaiah prefaced their request for prayer with what was probably a proverbial saying: "Children have come to the point of birth, and there is no strength to deliver them" (37:3, NASB). In other words, both mother and child—Jerusalem and her people—were staring death in the face. Their expectation of divine help was based on the blasphemous words of Rabshakeh, whom they accused of having been sent "to ridicule the living God" (37:4, NIV).

Isaiah responded to their appeal at once. He told them to take word to Hezekiah that help was on its way. He predicted that ultimately the Assyrian king, now threatening to destroy Jerusalem, would hear a rumor, return to his own land, and be killed (37:6–7).

When Sennacherib of Assyria attacked Palestine and the southern kingdom of Judah, he conquered the city of Lachish, some 35 miles southwest of Jerusalem. It was there he established his headquarters, and from there his armies moved north to Jerusalem. Looking ahead just a little (37:37–38), we see that after Sennacherib returned to Nineveh, he was killed by his own sons.

In the meantime, Sennacherib sent a second message to Hezekiah from Libnah, a frontier outpost some 10 miles north of Lachish (37:8–13). We are told that Sennacherib had withdrawn his troops from Lachish to Libnah when it was reported to him that the "king of Cush" (that is, Egypt) was advancing northward to attack him (37:8–9, ESV).

Sennacherib's message warned Hezekiah that he should not count on the Lord to protect him (37:10–13). After all, Sennacherib said, why should Hezekiah expect his God to do for him what the gods of other nations had been unable to do for them?

Hezekiah's response to this additional threat was to go directly to the Temple to pray. His prayer follows the pattern of the psalms of lament that occur so frequently in the book of Psalms. First, there is an opening invocation addressed to God (37:16–17); then follows a clear statement acknowledging Israel's peril (37:18–19). And Hezekiah closes his prayer with an urgent plea for deliverance: "But now Lord, our God, save us from his hand, so that all the kingdoms of the earth may know that You alone, Lord, are God" (37:20, NASB).

The answer to Hezekiah's prayer was relayed to him by the prophet Isaiah (37:21–35): Sennacherib would not attack Jerusalem. "'By the way that [Sennacherib] came, by the same he will return, and he will not come to this city,' declares the Lord. 'For I will protect this city to save it for My own sake, and for My servant David's sake'" (verses 34–35, NASB).

The order of these verses is sometimes hard to follow. It seems that verses 33–35 should follow immediately after verse 21. In the intervening verses, Zion, personified as a courageous young woman, sings of Sennacherib's doom (37:22–29; see also 10:5–19). Also included here is the promise of a sign to Hezekiah involving a three-year agricultural cycle and signifying that within a brief span of time the Assyrians will be gone and life will return to normal in the land of Judah (37:30–32; for other references to signs given to Judean kings, see 7:10–14; 38:7–8, 22).

Hezekiah's Illness and Recovery

All we can say with certainty about the date of Hezekiah's illness is that it occurred at a time when Jerusalem was being threatened by the king of Assyria (38:6). This could have been at any time between 705 and 701 BC. According to a later word (39:1), the envoys of the king of Babylon visited Hezekiah soon after his recovery, ostensibly to offer their congratulations for his improvement. Most scholars, however, believe they had another agenda. The real purpose of their visit, usually dated around 705 BC, was to enlist the support of Hezekiah in a rebellion against Assyria. According to this interpretation and the chronological order upon which it is based, Hezekiah's illness, noted in chapter 38, must have actually occurred before the events recorded in chapters 36–37.

Our scripture lesson at this point provides a classic example of the conditional nature of Hebrew prophecy. Hezekiah had become seriously ill ("to the point of death") and was told that he should set his house in order, for he would not recover (38:1, ESV). However, in response to the king's prayer (38:2–3), the word of doom was recalled, and Isaiah was sent the second time to tell him that an additional 15 years had been added to his life (38:4–5). The Old Testament clearly indicates that God's threats and promises are conditioned upon the response of the hearers (see Jeremiah 18:7–10).

The story of these events in the book of 2 Kings includes a note to the effect that the king also was told that within three days he would be sufficiently recovered to go up to the house of the Lord—the Temple (2 Kings 20:5). The Isaiah account of Hezekiah's illness omits any reference to this. However, both accounts record that Hezekiah asked for a sign to verify that the promised visit to the Temple would indeed take place (see Isaiah 38:22; 2 Kings 20:8).

In the Old Testament, signs are given for the purpose of validating the words of a prophet or of some other messenger sent from God (see Exodus 3:12; 4:1–9; Isaiah 7:10–14; 37:30–31; 38:7–8). The sign validating the Lord's promise to heal Hezekiah involved "turning the clock back," that is, causing the shadow on "the sun dial" to reverse directions and go backward ten degrees (38:8, KJV). More recent translations state that the shadow went back up "the ten steps it has gone down on the stairway of Ahaz" (NIV) to indicate the reversal of time—effectively using the steps as a form of sundial.

Chapter 38 concludes with Hezekiah's hymn of thanksgiving for restored health. This may have been composed to be sung on the occasion of his visit to the Temple three days after his recovery (see 2 Kings 20:5). It was common in Old Testament times for those who had been delivered from danger or catastrophe to go up to the Temple and there express their thanksgiving in song (see 1 Samuel 2:1–10; Psalms 18; 30; 34; 66; 116; Jonah 2:2–9).

The hymn opens with Hezekiah recounting his close brush with death (38:9–11). He describes death as the folding of the shepherd's tent or the severing of the weaver's threads (38:12). He meditates upon the fact that between sunrise and sunset his bones could all be broken and his fragile life cut off (38:13). In his great grief and melancholy, he can only appeal to the Lord for help (38:14), for it is the Lord Himself who has brought him to this sad state (38:15).

The rest of the hymn represents Hezekiah's reflections upon this harrowing experience after it had passed (38:17–20). God had not only rescued him from the jaws of death but also had forgiven his sins, putting even the memory of them behind Him (38:17). Hezekiah realized that if he had died, he would have had no further opportunity to praise God or to discover His truth (38:18). But now that his life had been spared, he would spend his days praising God and making known His truth to the next generation (38:19). In verse 20 it is suggested that Hezekiah wanted this hymn and other songs he had composed to be sung in the house of the Lord throughout all future generations. He had learned that praise is the most enduring testimony to God's saving power.

Hezekiah's Contact with the King of Babylon

The final section in the historical appendix to Isaiah's prophecies tells about Hezekiah's contact with Marduk-Baladan, the king of Babylon (39:1–8). This king, whose name meant "Marduk [the chief Babylonian god] has given a son," reigned over Babylon from 721 until 710 BC and again for a brief time after 705 BC. The interruptions in his reign can be explained by the fact that he was in constant conflict with the rulers of Assyria. But he was finally banished from power by Sennacherib of Assyria shortly after 705 BC.

The events in this part of our scripture lesson are usually dated shortly after 705 BC but before Sennacherib's defeat of Marduk-Baladan. Marduk-Baladan had sent messengers to Hezekiah under the pretext of congratulating him upon his recovery from illness (39:1), but the real purpose behind the visit was to draw Hezekiah into a coalition against Assyria. Hezekiah apparently pledged his cooperation, for he was willing for the messengers of the king of Babylon to inspect the supplies in his storehouse and the weapons in his arsenal (39:2). Judah was for all practical purposes a vassal of Assyria, and sharing this information with a power known to be hostile to Assyria was tantamount to rebellion.

We next read that Isaiah rebuked Hezekiah for his willingness to engage in such a risky undertaking (39:3–8). The prophet had consistently opposed Judah's dependence upon foreign alliances (see 7:3–9; 30:1–5, 15), and he saw no reason to change his mind at this stage in history. He even predicted to Hezekiah that in days to come the land of Judah would be devastated by the very nation that he was now willing to accept as his ally. Isaiah's prophecy was fulfilled just over a century later when Jerusalem and Judah were conquered by the Babylonians. The remainder of the book of Isaiah deals with the fortunes of the people of Israel following that fateful event.

Holy Lord, help me to be aware of friendships or associations that have the potential to lead me away from Your love. AMEN.

This is what the Lord, the God of your father David, says: I have heard your prayer and seen your tears.

—Isaiah 38:5 (NIV)

I was looking through past prayer requests in my daily journal when one entry stood out: *Please, Lord, give our family a brighter future!* I'd prayed that prayer for twelve straight years, years when we'd experienced one dark time after another. A marriage dissolved. Two grandchildren lost their father to a heart attack. Someone stopped communicating with other family members. Chronic health problems made life difficult for a young adult. Then Covid-19 hit, causing illness, lost work, and periods of isolation. Finances were uncertain. My husband, Don, died, and my time and energy were consumed with managing a rental property, farm, and finances.

As I read further into the journal, though, I made an amazing discovery. Many of my frantic prayers had already been answered. The sharp grief over separation and deaths eased. Family members affected by Covid-19 recovered and some jobs returned. My farm had an excellent corn crop. And there were blessings I hadn't asked for or anticipated. Son Patrick; his wife, Patricia; daughter Rebecca; and grandson Mark moved back to southwest Kansas, and having them close has kept me from being lonely. Grandson Caden won his county's 4-H Club pig show. Proceeds from selling the animal are helping with college expenses.

Our life circumstances aren't perfect. Health, work, and communication issues remain. But I'm thankful to God for giving us a brighter future on earth and a glimpse of the glories that await in heaven.

—*Penney Schwab*

Notes

Notes

LESSON 5: ISAIAH 40:1–45:25

Called to Comfort

Holy Lord, thank You for the comfort You bring me and for coming alongside to help me. Amen.

A span of over a century and a half separates chapters 39 and 40 of the book of Isaiah. Going from chapter 39 to chapter 40 is almost like closing one book and opening another. Chapter 40 and the remaining chapters of the book describe events that occurred after 587 BC, the date of Jerusalem's destruction and the beginning of the Babylonian exile.

This means that the world situation was entirely different. Following the destruction of Nineveh, the capital of Assyria, in 612 BC, the center of world power shifted to Babylon. Jerusalem also had been destroyed, and many of its citizens had been exiled to Babylon.

The Jewish exiles were for the most part a dispirited lot, brooding over the past and fearful for the future. Their discouragement could not be hidden, for they were saying, "My way is hidden from the Lord; my cause is disregarded by my God" (40:27, NIV). They also were saying, "The Lord has forsaken me, the Lord has forgotten me" (49:14, NIV). These were not isolated instances of complaining on the part of the exiles, as we see in Psalm 137 and Ezekiel 37:1–14. The Jews were a people without a country, and their future looked dark indeed.

The troubles of the Jewish exiles were real and not imaginary. They had been deported from Judah to Babylon because of their persistent rebellion against the Lord (see 42:22–25), rebellion that is noted by the historian (see 2 Kings 24:1–4) and condemned by the prophets (see Jeremiah 17:1–4; 25:8–11; Ezekiel 5:5–11). Their captors had shown them no mercy but had treated them harshly as their time in Babylon dragged on for almost 50 years (see 47:5–6). The Isaiah writer makes it clear, though, that it wasn't God's will for His people to experience such oppression, but they were suffering the consequences of their own actions in having abandoned the way of peace God offered them (see 48:17–19).

Their troubles were many and deep; however, the Lord had not forgotten them, even though they often felt that He had (see 49:14–16). In fact, God was preparing a deliverer of the Jewish refugees in the person of Cyrus, the king of Persia. Although this pagan king did not even know God (see 45:1–4), nevertheless he would be God's agent for liberating the exiles and His instrument for rebuilding Jerusalem and its Temple (see 44:28; 2 Chronicles 36:22–23; Ezra 1:1–4; 6:1–5).

Out of the midst of the gloom of the exile, a prophet arises to speak the words of comfort and hope found in these last chapters of the book of Isaiah. Because of the strong message of encouragement found here, these chapters have been called "the book of consolation." Others have referred to them as "the heart of the Old Testament." Because of this prophet's clear teaching about vicarious suffering, the love and compassion of God for Israel, and God's universal purpose for all humankind, he has been called "the Evangelist of the Old Testament." The title is certainly appropriate, since he was always talking about proclaiming good news (see 40:9; 41:27; 52:7; 61:1; 65:17–18).

Before we move in for a closer look at these chapters, it is important to note the style and form in which they are written. The form is poetic, as can be seen in almost any modern translation, with its short and alternating indented lines. It can be argued that the poetry of these chapters ranks with the best that has ever been written in any language. It is no wonder that many of the themes of Handel's *Messiah* were borrowed from these chapters. Clearly the words of this prophet were meant to be sung.

The form of these chapters, especially chapters 40–55, is more like a symphony than a formal treatise on biblical theology. This explains why it is practically impossible to outline their contents. Here certain themes are first announced and then repeated in a variety of different arrangements. The whole composition reaches a climax in chapter 53, with chapters 54 and 55 serving as the postlude.

Some of the major themes found in this part of Isaiah are these:

- The incomparable greatness of Israel's God, who is both Lord of creation and Lord of history (see 40:12–17, 21–26; 44:6–8; 45:5–7)
- The utter folly of idol worship (see 40:18–20; 41:5–7; 44:9–20; 45:16; 46:1–2, 5–7)

- Encouragement to a nation in despair (see 40:1–2, 9–11, 27–31; 41:10–13; 43:1–2; 51:1–8)
- The day of the Lord as a day of salvation, celebration, and victory (see 40:3–5; 43:14–21; 52:1–12; 54:1–3; 55:12–13)
- The mission of the Servant of the Lord (see 42:1–7; 43: 10–13; 49:1–6; 50:4–9; 52:13–53:12; 61:1–3)
- The universal purpose of God for all humankind (see 45:22–24; 49:6; 60:1–3)

Comfort for Discouraged People (40:1–31)

Called to Be a Comforter

This part of the book of Isaiah opens with God's call to the prophet to undertake a mission of comfort to His discouraged people (40:1–8), who were not only separated from their homeland but also felt alienated from God (see 40:27; 49:14; Psalm 137; Ezekiel 37:1–14). In fact, they wondered if God would ever be willing to forgive them and receive them back into His fellowship.

The opening words of chapter 40 set the stage for the chapters that follow. The prophet is told, "'Comfort, comfort My people,' says your God" (40:1, NASB). The comfort God wanted them to receive was the good news that He had forgiven all their sins and was about to restore them to their homeland. Furthermore, God assured them, He was more than satisfied that they had been sufficiently punished for all their wrongdoings (40:2).

In all of this, God made it clear that their sins of disobedience had been serious. They had indeed failed Him, and they had no one to blame for their failure except themselves (see 42:24–25). But now that they had paid such a high cost for their failure, God was ready to receive them back into His fellowship. His willingness to forgive becomes a recurring theme throughout these chapters (see 54:7–8).

With awesome grandeur and poetic imagery, the prophet next speaks of an unidentified voice "of one calling, 'In the wilderness prepare the way for the LORD, make straight in the desert a highway for our God. Every valley shall be raised up, every mountain and hill made low; the rough ground shall become level, the rugged places a plain'" (40:3–4, NIV). In other words, every obstacle was to be removed and a safe way prepared for the exiles' return to Judah. The voice went on to tell that "the glory of the LORD shall be revealed, and all flesh shall see it together, for the mouth of the LORD has spoken" (40:5, ESV). The words "all flesh shall see it" in this fifth verse speak of the inclusiveness of God's love and grace. "The glory of the LORD" is for everyone, everywhere!

The Strong Word of God

When the prophet heard the instructions to give the people of Israel God's message of comfort, he exclaimed in despair, "What shall I call out?" And he is answered with, "All flesh is grass, and all its loveliness is like the flower of the field. . . . The people are indeed grass!" (40:6–7, NASB). He was neither the first nor the last prophet to be discouraged by the instability and fickleness of his audience.

But then the voice continued, "The grass withers, the flower fades, but the word of our God stands forever" (40:8, NASB).

In this response to the prophet's question, we find recognition of the weakness of people, who wither as easily as grass. But there is also a proclamation of the power of the Word of God, which will continue to stand after grass has withered and flowers have faded. In this forceful statement, the prophet is told to look beyond the frailty of people to the enduring power of the Word of God; then he will have no cause for fear (40:8; see 55:10–11).

The Strength and Gentleness of God

Next comes the good news to the exiles and to the people of Jerusalem and Judah that God had not forgotten them but was about to return to them in triumph (40:9). They thought that when the Temple was destroyed, He had left them (see Ezekiel 11:23), but now they are told that He will be with them. He "comes with power, and he rules with a mighty arm"—like a mighty warrior (40:10, NIV), but then He goes on to say, "He tends his flock like a shepherd: he gathers the lambs in his arms and carries them close to his heart (40:11, NIV). What is emphasized here is His strength and His gentleness. The two are not contradictory but complementary.

This has special meaning for us because all our questions about God can be reduced to two: Is He able? Does He care? To believe in a god who was loving and compassionate, yet powerless to act, would leave us with a feeling of helplessness in life's struggles. On the other hand, to believe in a god whose power and might were absolute, but who was also unloving and unmoved by our hurts, would plunge us into despair.

The Matchless Power of God

The writer next expands on the idea of God's power and might (40:12–26). In those ancient times, war was not only a conflict between two nations; it was also thought the conflict was between the gods of those nations. This meant that the gods of the winner were considered superior to those of the loser. To counteract any possibility that the defeated and discouraged Jews might think the Babylonian gods were superior to the Lord God, the prophet now gives vivid testimony to the greatness of the Creator-God of Israel (40:12–14).

Then, immediately following this marvelous testimony as to the greatness of their God, he denigrates the human-made gods of the pagan nations (40:15–20). With descriptive color the writer says, "Behold, the nations are as a drop of a bucket, and are counted as the small dust of the balance [scales]" (40:15, KJV). This certainly doesn't mean that God is indifferent to the pagan nations, because one of the main features of this prophecy is its universality (see 45:22; 49:6; 56:6–8). The point being made is that these pagan nations don't pose a threat to either God or His people.

We note here and in other places that the writer enjoyed poking fun at idol makers and idol worshippers. The first example of this occurs in this part of our scripture lesson (40:18–20; see also 41:5–7; 44:9–20; 46:5–7). We see here that in idolatrous nations both the rich and the poor have their idols. The idols of the rich are made of expensively carved wood overlaid with silver and gold (40:19). The poor, on the other hand, must be content with wooden idols that can be made cheaply (40:20).

These idols, however, cannot be compared to Israel's God. He is the Lord of creation and the Lord of history (40:21–26). More than any other part of the Old Testament, the prophecies found in chapters 40–55 of Isaiah magnify the Lord as Creator. The verb translated "to create" occurs a total of sixteen times within these chapters (see 41:4; 44:6; 48:12). Interestingly enough, it occurs only eleven times in Genesis. Wherever this verb occurs in the Old Testament, it always has God as its subject—that One who performs the action.

Because Isaiah 40–55 belongs to the latter part of the Babylonian exile, the references to God as Creator take on added significance for two reasons. First, the Babylonians had an elaborate creation myth attributing the creation to their god Marduk. The Jewish exiles needed to be warned against accepting this as truth. Second, the Hebrew exiles needed to be reminded that if their God had power to create and sustain the universe, He surely would be able to deliver them from the Babylonians.

The urgent questions asked in verse 21—"Do you not know? Do you not hear?" (ESV)—are intended to rouse the Israelites from their spiritual lethargy and to call them back to the roots of their faith. They are to remember that their God sits enthroned above the circle of the earth (40:22; see also Psalms 2:4; 9:7; 29:10), and from His elevated position the people of the earth appear as grasshoppers (40:22; see also Numbers 13:33). He stretches out the heavens as easily as a nomad might unfold his tent in preparation for making camp (40:22).

How easy it is for people who live in a nation as rich and as strong as ours to forget that our destiny rests ultimately in the hands of God. Arnold Toynbee, the late author, philosopher, and historian, taught that when nations prosper and begin to feel self-sufficient, they fall into moral decay. According to his reckoning, there have been twenty-one world civilizations during the course of human history. Each of these has followed a pattern involving four stages: birth, growth, internal decay, final collapse. Toynbee also notes that civilizations collapse not because of external pressures but because of internal decay. Could it be that we also will take our place in the graveyard of dead civilizations? Don't forget that God is still in control of history!

The prophet next goes on to point out that as the controller of history, the Lord reduces the rulers of the earth to nothing—even the mighty princes and judges of Babylon. "They shall wither, and the whirlwind shall take them away as stubble" (40:24, KJV). Then the prophet rises to lofty heights as he makes the point that Israel's God is in complete control of the stars in the heavens (40:26). This was an important point because the Babylonians made astrology and star worship a vital part of their religion. They not only considered the stars to be divine, but they also believed the movement of the stars determined their destiny. So, in poetic language, the prophet strikes at the very heart of the Babylonian religion as he strips the stars of magical power and divinity and reduces them to the rank of privates in the Lord's army. He speaks as though the heavens were but a parade ground where the starry hosts are assembled each evening for roll call. Not one is missing, not one fails to report for duty. Seen in its Babylonian setting, this was a strong refutation of idolatry and a call for Israel to worship and obey the Lord alone.

The Sustainer of the Weary

When the prophet talked of God's power and mercy, his listeners were highly skeptical, because there was so much in their situation that seemed to contradict this. How could they possibly believe that God reigned over creation and history when they were exiled to Babylon and when Jerusalem still lay in ruins? The world often faces this problem. How can we believe that God is king when the forces of evil seem to be enthroned on every hand? Where is God when bad things happen to good people?

In response to the prophet, the Israelites complained that God was no longer interested in their welfare or in seeing justice done on their behalf (40:27). The long years of exile had plunged them into despair. But the prophet answers their complaint with one of the finest confessions of faith to be found in the Bible. He tells them in effect that their concept of God is far too small. "Do you not know? Have you not heard? The Everlasting God, the LORD, the Creator of the ends of the earth does not become weary or tired. His understanding is unsearchable" (40:28, NASB). These words were spoken by one who had himself gone through the valley of despair before emerging into the sunlight of faith (40:6–8).

It wasn't enough, however, for the people of Israel to be told that God was strong, while they were so pitifully weak. They also needed to be told that God stood ready to share His great strength with them. And that is precisely the message of verse 29: "He gives strength to the weary and increases the power of the weak" (NIV). For us to be told that God never faints or grows weary (40:28) is not nearly so encouraging as to be told that He offers power to us whenever we are ready to give up. The prophet then says that God's strength is absolutely indispensable, because human strength, no matter how lusty and vigorous it may be, will ultimately fail us. Even the very young need a strength beyond their own (verse 30).

God offers us His power, but how do we make contact with it? How do we receive it? The prophet's answer is that God's strength is made available to those who learn to wait on Him. As a matter of fact, the Isaiah writer at this point is at his poetic best when he says, "They will soar on wings like eagles; they will run and not grow weary, they will walk and not be faint" (40:31, NIV). These words rang with power in the sixth century BC, and their promise and authenticity will take God's people through the twenty-first century and beyond. Learning to wait upon the Lord is one of life's most important lessons (see 49:23; 51:5; 64:4; and Psalms 25:3, 21; 27:14; 33:20; 37:7, 9; 40:1).

But what does it mean to wait upon the Lord? The Hebrew word translated "to wait" has an interesting history. Its basic meaning is "to wind," "to twist," or "to weave." The nouns for "cord" and "spider's web" come from this same root. So, "to wait upon the Lord" means to let Him become our hope, our cord of escape, our lifeline.

There's more, though. The verb means "to wait eagerly, expectantly." When it is used in Psalms 56:6 and 119:95 it describes the breathless waiting of those who lie in ambush to slay their enemies. And when it is used in Isaiah 5:4–7, it describes the farmer's eager waiting for his crops to mature. This series of pictures—the tension of the stretched cord, the warrior waiting in ambush, and the farmer anticipating the harvest—illustrates the richness of this word.

The promise is certain: To those who learn to wait upon the Lord, He gives His own unfailing strength. This is what is meant by the promise that they shall "*renew* their strength" (40:31, NIV; italics added for emphasis). Actually, "change" or "exchange" would be a more accurate translation than "renew." Those who wait upon the Lord do more than simply "renew" their strength; they exchange their faltering strength for God's unfailing strength. Their strength comes from the everlasting God, the Creator of the universe, who never faints or grows weary.

The prophet then describes the outcome of waiting upon the Lord. The verbs in this verse may seem to be arranged in reverse order. Waiting upon the Lord is compared first to flying, then to running, and finally to walking. If this is progress, then it seems to be progress downhill! If there were a fourth step, it would probably be crawling!

But is this not an apt description of the life of faith? Occasionally, we may indeed soar on wings of faith. From time to time, we may run without growing weary. But most of the time, we simply plod along through life. And the real test of our endurance comes not when we soar on eagle's wings, or run like a trained athlete, but when we are simply called upon to put one foot before the other and keep marching, minute by minute, hour by hour. It is in our ordinary, everyday life that our faith is most severely tested.

The prophet's message was important to the people in his day, but it is profoundly important to us in our Christian pilgrimage. Most of us sag under the pressures and pace of our busy, stressful lives. There is an appalling lack of joy and enthusiasm in our lives. The causes of our weariness are not unrelated to those the prophet encountered among the Hebrew exiles in Babylon. Like them, we often carry a burden of unforgiven sin and unresolved guilt. Like them, we don't really rely on the Word of God as a living force in our daily lives. Like them, we are tempted to abandon God and go after the easy "idols" of our modern world. Like them, we have lost faith in the power of God and in His purpose in history. Is it any wonder that we faint and grow weary?

The cure for our condition is the same now as it was in the sixth century BC: become acutely aware of the presence and the power of God in our midst. Captive Israel—the captive church—still waits for a prophetic voice to proclaim, "Behold your God!"

Cyrus and the New Exodus (41:1–29)

The prophet continues now to further expand on the theme that God alone shapes and controls the outcome of history. His ultimate goal is the establishment of His rule over all of the people and nations of the earth (see 45:23; Habakkuk 2:14; Revelation 11:15). History is not governed by chance or by the nation that possesses the largest armies. We are a part of "His-story," and the final outcome is never in doubt. Hymn writer Maltbie Davenport Babcock expressed it well when he wrote:

This is my Father's world,
Oh, let me ne'er forget,
That though the wrong seems oft so strong,
God is the Ruler yet.

The Isaiah writer now takes us into a courtroom scene in which God summons the pagan nations to appear before Him so that He can demonstrate the absolute ineffectiveness of their gods. The point is clearly made that with the demise of their gods, those nations will be ineffective in preventing the fulfillment of God's purpose for His people.

A Liberator from the East

The trial scene opens with the Lord Himself calling for the people and rulers all across the world to silently listen to the word of the Lord (41:1). They also were told to "renew their strength," an obvious reference to the same phrase used earlier (40:31). Here, though, it seems to be used in derision, suggesting that they would need great strength to withstand God's judgment.

Next the prophet shows his fondness for using questions designed not so much to obtain information as to instruct his audience (41:2–4; see also 40:12–14, 18, 21, 27–28; 42:19, 23–24; 49:15). The key question here is, "Who has performed and done this, calling forth [and guiding the destinies of] the generations [of the nations] from the beginning?" The answer is provided by the Lord Himself: "I, the Lord—the first, and with the last [existing before history began, the ever-present, unchanging God]—I am He" (41:4, AMP). The clear meaning of this response is that the great "I Am," who appeared to Moses at the burning bush, even now is raising up a new deliverer and preparing to set His exiled people free through a second exodus.

But who is this deliverer God has raised up? The overwhelming evidence points to Cyrus, king of Persia, although he is not mentioned by name until later (44:28). Cyrus was only an insignificant king in Asia Minor until he annexed the territory of Media in 550 BC. He went on to conquer Croesus (KREE-suss), the fabled wealthy king of Lydia, in 546 BC. His apparently irresistible progress in expanding his territory struck fear in the hearts of the rulers of Babylon. At the same time, it raised the hopes of the Hebrew exiles that their liberation might be near. These hopes were fulfilled when Cyrus conquered Babylon in 539 BC and permitted the exiles to return to Jerusalem and Judah. The prophet's words here probably should be dated after 550 BC, the beginning of Cyrus's rise to power, but before 539 BC, the date of Cyrus's conquest of Babylon.

The prophet also makes the astonishing claim that it was the Lord who launched Cyrus on his victorious career and made the nations of the ancient Near East powerless to oppose him (41:2–4; see also 45:1–4, 13–14). God's purpose was not to exalt Cyrus but to bring about the liberation of His people and the restoration of Jerusalem and its Temple (see 44:28).

Widespread Panic

The Isaiah writer then tells us that Cyrus's victories threw the nations of the ancient Near East into a state of panic (41:5–7). They met together in conferences to map their strategy, but the only solution they could think of was to manufacture more potent gods.

This was the second time the prophet had ridiculed all human-made gods (see 40:18–20; 44:9–20; 46:1–7). His description of the workmen trying desperately to encourage one another provides a touch of comic relief (41:7). The prophet knew that all their hammering and nailing wouldn't make any difference, for nothing could stop Cyrus until he had accomplished God's purpose for him and the world.

Comfort to Captive Israel

Next, turning his attention to the discouraged exiles in Babylon, the prophet offers reassurance (41:8–16). They are told first of all that they are still God's chosen people (41:8–10). This assurance was important because many Judeans felt that their exile in Babylon signaled the end of God's covenant with them. But the Lord says, "So do not fear, for I am with you; do not be dismayed, for I am your God. I will strengthen you and help you; I will uphold you with my righteous right hand" (41:10, NIV). What a thrill those electric words must have been to those discouraged, displaced Judeans in Babylon! These same words have brought encouragement to the people of God from Isaiah's time to ours.

Before going on, though, take notice of the title given to the exiles and the people of Israel in verses 8 and 9. Here for the first time in the book of Isaiah, Israel is referred to as the Lord's servant (see also 42:1, 19; 43:10; 44:1, 2, 21, 26; 45:4; 49:3, 5–7; 50:10; 52:13; 53:11). However, this title should not be interpreted in a servile sense; in Old Testament times the "servant of the king" was someone whom the king appointed to administer his affairs and to function as his personal representative. Furthermore, the fact that God speaks of such persons as Abraham (Genesis 26:24), Moses (Numbers 12:7–8), and David (2 Samuel 3:18) as His servants shows that this is primarily a title of honor.

Next, the Hebrews are further encouraged by being told that none of their enemies will prevail against them (41:11–16). Because of all that has happened, even though they see themselves as lowly worms (41:14), they are assured that God sees them as a mighty sledge, capable of threshing the mountains and turning the hills into chaff (41:15). The mountains and hills referred to here represent the pagan nations now oppressing Israel. But then comes the good news: the people of Israel will win out over them (41:16).

In verse 14, God refers to Himself as Israel's Redeemer. This is one of the most significant titles for God in the Scriptures. Although it never appears in the first thirty-nine chapters of Isaiah, it occurs thirteen times in chapters 40–66 (see 43:14; 44:6, 24; 47:4; 48:17; 49:7, 26; 54:5, 8; 59:20; 60:16; 63:16). The only other prophet to apply this title to God is Jeremiah, and he does so only once (Jeremiah 50:34). The verb translated "to redeem" is also used often in the latter part of Isaiah (see 43:1; 44:22–23; 48:20). And another form of the verb is used three times to designate Israel as the redeemed people of God (51:10; 62:12; 63:4).

The word *redeemer* is a technical term drawn from family law in ancient Israel. The redeemer in everyday life was a near-kinsman charged with certain family responsibilities. When a close relative was forced by poverty to sell himself into slavery, the "redeemer" was under obligation to bail him out (see Leviticus 25:47–54). When the relative, because of poverty, had to sell his ancestral land, the "redeemer" was responsible for buying the mortgage and seeing that the land stayed within the family or clan (see Leviticus 25:25).

A special responsibility of the kinsman-redeemer was to marry the childless widow of a deceased brother in order to guarantee that there would be children to carry on his brother's name (see Genesis 38:7–8; Deuteronomy 25:4–10; Ruth 2:20; 3:12; 4:1–12). Finally, the redeemer was under obligation to avenge the blood of a murdered kinsman (see Numbers 35:16–21; Joshua 20:1–6). Blood vengeance rested on the twofold principle of the sacredness of blood (Genesis 9:4–6) and of the solidarity of the tribe or family. The Hebrews fully accepted the principle that no one is an island unto himself or herself.

Consequently, to speak of God as Israel's Redeemer introduced a daring concept. It meant, first of all, that the bonds that linked Israel to God and God to Israel were as intimate and as enduring as family ties. Next, it meant that no price was too great for God to pay for the redemption of His people (see 43:3–4; 54:5–8). Finally, it meant that the exalted God—the Holy One—whose throne is above the heavens, is also the God who stoops down to help those who are lowly and oppressed.

Centuries before, God had told Moses that He had seen the affliction of His people in Egypt, had heard their cry, and had come down to redeem them from the hand of their oppressors (Exodus 3:7–8). God also came down in the person of His Son and our Savior, Jesus Christ, to redeem us from the bondage of sin and death. We can only say with the Apostle Paul, "Thanks be unto God for his unspeakable gift" (2 Corinthians 9:15, KJV), for even today He "comes down" to be with us.

The Wilderness Road

The Isaiah writer now gives us a lovely poem in which Israel's deliverance from Babylon is described as a journey along a wilderness road (41:17–20). In highly symbolic language the prophet pictures the miracles that would occur along this journey as outstripping those that took place in the first exodus from Egypt. In the first exodus, the sea was parted and became dry land (Exodus 14:21–22). In the new exodus, it would be as if God had reversed this process, changing the wilderness into a pool and the dry land into springs of water (41:17–18). The prophet also speaks symbolically of the wilderness being transformed into a kind of botanical garden, filled with all kinds of useful and beautiful trees (41:19–20). Throughout chapters 40–66, nature is seen as being alive and able to participate in the events surrounding the people's return from exile (see 43:16–21; 48:20–21; 49:9–11; 55:12–13; 65:25).

Impotence and Omnipotence

Next the prophet returns to the theme of God's superiority over all pagan idols (41:21–29). In satirical language he challenges the idols to prove that they are gods by three tests: (1) Can they interpret the underlying significance of events that occurred in the past (41:22)? The "former things" probably include all God's mighty acts from the time of Moses to the time of Cyrus. (2) Can they predict events that still lie in the future (41:22–23)? (3) Can they intervene in human history either to do good or to do ill (41:23)?

The Holy One of Israel issued the challenge, and the idols flunked the test. They are impotent, and therefore can do nothing (41:24). The last half of verse 24 contrasts God's choice of Israel (see 41:8–9) with the pagan people's choice of idols. Idols never choose; they must always be chosen. This is true with our twenty-first-century idols of power and material gain.

God passes the tests the idols failed. He will intervene to change the course of world history by raising up Cyrus, who will overcome all opposition (41:25–26). Cyrus also will become a bearer of good news to Jerusalem (41:27)—a probable reference to his decree for the rebuilding of the city (see 44:28). In a parting shot, derision is directed to the impotent and useless pagan gods as they are referred to as nothing more than "molten images" full of "wind and confusion" (41:28–29, KJV).

The Servant of the Lord (42:1–25)

As we move into this part of our scripture lesson, we come to the first of what Bible scholars often call Servant Songs (42:1–4). Others are found in 49:1–6; 50:4–9; and 52:13–53:12. Some interpreters have suggested that 61:1–3 should be added to this list. These verses describe the special mission of one who is called the servant of the Lord.

The Mission of the Servant

God is the speaker in the first Servant Song. He describes the servant as one in whom He is pleased, and one upon whom He has placed His Spirit (42:1). The servant is the Lord's "elect," which means he has been chosen for a particular mission, and that mission is defined as bringing forth "justice" to the Gentiles (42:1, most translations).

Question: How does the servant perform his mission? First, he doesn't cry out or cause his voice to be heard in the street (42:2). This does not mean he is a "silent witness." The verb translated "to cry out" is always used elsewhere in the Old Testament to describe the urgent cry of the oppressed for relief (see Genesis 4:10; Exodus 3:7; Judges 4:3; Psalm 107:6; Isaiah 19:20). It means here that the Lord will protect him so that he will have no need to cry out in distress.

Then we're told that the servant will exercise a pastoral role, neither breaking the "bruised reed" nor snuffing out the "smoldering wick" (42:3, NIV). This verse may make reference to an ancient courtroom practice in which the accused is declared guilty by having his staff broken and his oil lamp extinguished. The servant's role is not to condemn but to pardon.

This emphasizes our responsibility toward the weak and bruised in our society. No better model could be found for this quality of ministry than that provided by Jesus. Not only did He refuse to condemn a fallen woman (John 8:1–10), but He also freely associated with all social and religious outcasts. He was the friend of tax collectors and sinners.

Next the writer suggests that the servant is exposed to the same dangers as those to whom he ministers (42:4). He takes his place beside those to whom he ministers and identifies with them in their weakness and suffering. This is the first intimation that the servant is to become a "suffering servant," a thought that is fully developed in the later Servant Songs.

The final point that is emphasized in the first Servant Song is that the servant endures all trials and emerges victorious in the end. He will not fail or be discouraged. He will establish justice in the world, and "the coastlands" (NASB), or "the islands" (NIV)—representing the nations of the world near and far—will "wait expectantly" (NASB) for or "put their hope" (NIV) in his law (42:4). Through the servant, God's plan of salvation is seen on a global scale (42:5–9).

A New Song of Deliverance

The "new things" referred to in verse 9 introduce a "new song" (42:10–17), a grand hymn of praise. The word "new" is a key concept in chapters 40–66 of Isaiah (see 41:15; 42:9–10; 43:19; 48:6; 62:2; 65:17; 66:22), although it never occurs earlier in the book. It describes the appearance of something previously unknown and totally unexpected.

The writer says that the inhabitants of distant foreign nations, along with desert tribes close at hand, are to praise the Lord in song (42:10–12) because of God's deliverance of His captive and exiled people (42:13–17). Then, with the deliverance of His people from captivity in Babylon, assurance is given that the Lord will guide them as they travel into their future.

God's people in all times have been able to live in the confidence of the Lord's guidance. This was beautifully expressed by the Psalmist when he wrote, "I [God] will instruct you and teach you in the way which you should go; I will advise you with My eye upon you" (Psalm 32:8, NASB). And as Christians, we can make our way through each day with Jesus's assurance, "When the Spirit of truth comes, he will guide you into all the truth" (John 16:13, ESV).

When Servants Do Not Serve

The Isaiah writer next takes up a theme that runs throughout these chapters: the failure of the Israelites to be faithful servants of the Lord (42:18–25). He accuses them of still being blind and deaf in their disobedience of the Lord even though He has delivered them time and time again from their enemies (42:20–25). Despite their stubbornness and disobedience, we see the Lord here continuing to refer to them as "my servant." What a magnificent picture of the grace of God!

God of the Past and Present (43:1–28)

The mood of the Isaiah writer changes abruptly as he says, "*But now,* this is what the LORD says, He who is your Creator, Jacob, and He who formed you, Israel: 'Do not fear, for I have redeemed you; I have called you by name; you are Mine!'" (43:1, NASB; italics added for emphasis). In moving into this salvation prophecy, the people are reminded that God was not only the God of the past, but He is also the God of the present. The great exodus experience that loomed so large in Israel's past was about to be repeated. As God had liberated them from Egypt under the leadership of Moses, so He now would liberate them from Babylon by the hand of Cyrus (see 44:24–28). And of this we can be sure: the victory celebration beside the Red Sea (see Exodus 15:1–21) was nothing compared to what would take place when Israel leaves Babylon: "The ransomed of the LORD shall return and come to Zion with singing; everlasting joy shall be upon their heads; they shall obtain gladness and joy, and sorrow and sighing shall flee away" (Isaiah 35:10, ESV; italics added for emphasis; see also 49:8–13; 52:7–12; 55:12–13).

Amazing Grace

Following God's assurance in verse 1 that He is their Redeemer and that they are His people, He gives them these remarkable words of promise: "When you pass through the waters, I will be with you; and when you pass through the rivers, they will not sweep over you. When you walk through the fire, you will not be burned; the flames will not set you ablaze. For I am the LORD your God, the Holy One of Israel, your Savior" (43:2–3, NIV).

With this uplifting pronouncement, God was assuring His people in all time that their future was secure. Yes, they would confront difficulties. Yes, the way wouldn't always be easy. But through fire and water and adversity, God would be with them. They could count on Him. It was true that their sin and disobedience had led to slavery and exile, but now they would be liberated. They would be free!

Effective Witnessing

Briefly then, the writer returns to the courtroom setting as God makes it clear that because of all He has done for them, they are to be His witnesses (43:8–13). But their witnessing must be more than words; it involved service. As God's witnesses, we are to demonstrate our love for Him by our care and concern for others. It is our "walk" that gives meaning to our "talk."

A New Exodus

After reminding the people of Israel of how He delivered them on the occasion of the exodus out of Egypt (43:16–17), the Lord now tells them to forget that first deliverance and concentrate on the new exodus that is about to occur (43:19–20), and for which He should receive praise (43:20–21).

Unrepentant

Chapter 43 closes on a rather sad note. In spite of all that has happened, the Israelites are still unrepentant. Their years in exile seem to have taught them little. They are neglectful and fail to honor the Lord with their sacrifices. Furthermore, they are continuing in their sinful ways and are listening to rebellious teachers (43:22–27). At a time when their spiritual condition should have been at a peak, they were disobedient to the heavenly vision that was theirs.

Yet even here there is a word of hope as the Lord says, "I, I alone, am the one who wipes out your wrongdoings for My own sake, and I will not remember your sins" (43:25, NASB). Again—amazing grace—while the people of Israel are undeserving, God still forgives because that's the way He is!

No God but the Lord (44:1–27)

Spiritual Renewal

Chapter 44 opens with "But now" and goes on to tell "Jacob" (Israel) that, in spite of all that has happened, God gives His people the desperately needed word of assurance and promise of renewal (44:1–5). His assurance comes in giving them a new name, Jeshurun—footnoted in the Amplified Version as "Israel, the upright one" (verse 2). This unusual name appears four times in the Hebrew Bible. Even as the deceitful Jacob was given a new identity when his name was changed to Israel, now the people of Israel were given a new identity as upright ones. And with the new name would come refreshment and renewed commitment (44:3–5).

God and Pagan Gods

The Isaiah writer next gives us a brief prophecy dealing with the Lord's claim of being the one and only God. The names applied to Him here are significant also. He is called Lord, King of Israel, Redeemer, and "the LORD of hosts," "the LORD Almighty," or "the LORD of armies" (44:6, KJV, NIV, and NASB, respectively). Here, too, is the Lord's sole claim to deity: "I am the first, and I am the last" (KJV). Only Israel's God can predict the future, and because of all He is, there is no reason to be fearful of the pagan gods (44:7–8).

And with this declaration, the prophet then presents a long satire against idolatry (44:9–20). This lengthy satire is not directed at the Babylonians who made their own gods—it is for the Jewish exiles who may have been tempted to worship those pagan gods.

Most of us in the modern world would be very critical of anyone guilty of worshipping an idol or false god. Yet an idol need not be made from stone or wood; it is anything devised by the human mind or shaped by human hands that is a substitute for God. The essence of idolatry is setting something less than God in the place of God. And that "something" can be family, position, material gain, power—anything or anyone that we put ahead of God in our daily lives.

Remember These Things and Praise God

Next follow five great affirmations that God gives His people, words of assurance to live by: (1) "You, Israel, are my servant" (44:21); (2) "I have made you" (44:21); (3) "I will not forget you" (44:21); (4) "I have swept away . . . your sins" (44:22); (5) "I have redeemed you" (44:22, NIV). After these breathtaking affirmations the prophet offers a glorious hymn of praise to the miracle-working God (44:23–27).

Cyrus, the Agent of God's Purpose (44:28–45:25)

The rise of Cyrus, the Persian, was one of the most significant events in ancient history. He brought the mighty Babylonian Empire to an end and founded an empire of his own that lasted for more than two centuries. Cyrus influenced many subsequent leaders, such as Alexander the Great, Julius Caesar, and Thomas Jefferson, and thus helped shape history for hundreds of years, with consequences that are still felt today.

The Lord's Shepherd and Anointed One

The first time Cyrus is mentioned by name in Isaiah is in 44:28. Here he is called the Lord's shepherd, and the one through whom the divine purpose will be performed (44:28–45:8). This applies specifically to the future rebuilding of Jerusalem and the Temple.

The Persian ruler is also addressed as the Lord's anointed (45:1). This is a title applied elsewhere in the Old Testament to priests (see Leviticus 4:3, 5, 16; 6:15), to kings (see 1 Samuel 24:6, 10; Psalm 2:2), and, in a metaphorical sense, to patriarchs (see Psalm 105:15).

Cyrus is the only Gentile who is given this title. It describes someone who was given a special mission in relationship to Israel. The title was therefore appropriate to Cyrus because the Lord had raised him up to destroy Babylon and to free the Hebrews to return home. Although it later came to be used in a technical sense to refer to the coming Messiah as God's "Anointed One," it must not be given this meaning here. Cyrus was given an important mission but should never be considered the Lord's Messiah.

More emphasis is given to that which the Lord would do for Cyrus than to that which Cyrus would do for the Lord (45:1–3). He would take his right hand and lead him on a path of victory, opening for him the gates of fortified cities and enabling him to seize their treasures. All this God would do for the sake of His people Israel (45:4). He did this through the instrumentality of one who does not even know Him (45:4). God's power is such that He can use world rulers to carry out His purposes even when they do not know Him and are unaware that they are serving Him.

Two themes are interwoven throughout this section: God's choice of Cyrus and the uniqueness of God. In no other part of Scripture is the belief in one God (monotheism) more clearly stated than here. Even His choice of Cyrus is in order that all may know that He alone is God (45:6).

Since this prophet believes so strongly that there is one God and only one, there is no room in his theology for even a trace of dualism. For him the Lord is the Creator of both light and darkness, of both good and evil (45:7). The reference to evil here is not to moral evil but to afflictions, calamities, and adversities.

On the other hand, the Persians believed in two creator-gods. The first, Ahura-Mazda, was creator of light and goodness, while the second, Ahriman, was creator of darkness and evil. The prophet refutes this dualistic view of the universe by affirming that everything in existence owes its origin to God alone (45:7). According to this view, God is the supreme and only cause in the universe, and He reigns without a rival.

The Potter and the Clay

The prophet next gives us a parable of the potter and the clay (45:9–13). This seems to be addressed to certain Jews who objected to the idea of God's working through a pagan king to accomplish His purposes. In the parable they are told that the clay has no right to challenge the potter, even as children have no right to challenge their fathers or their mothers (45:9–10). In other words, there may be times when the end does justify the means, and this was the case with Cyrus. God intended to work through him for the restoration of the exiles (45:13). Israel is to be redeemed "not for price nor reward" (45:13, KJV)—redemption is God's free gift to an undeserving people.

The Savior of All Nations

As the prophet foresees Cyrus's swift victory over Babylon and the return of the Jews to their homeland, he looks beyond this to a time when God will be acknowledged as the Savior of all nations (45:14). He believed that God's purposes ultimately involved much more than just the return of the Jewish exiles and the rebuilding of Jerusalem—there was a worldwide purpose.

The prophet sees a time when all people will swear allegiance to God. At that time God will make Himself known to everyone, and Israel will be delivered (45:15–17). No indication is given as to when all this would take place, but for now, it is still an unfulfilled dream.

Next, we see that God's purpose in redemption encompasses even the physical universe (45:18–19). He did not create the world to be a chaos, an uninhabited wasteland. Rather, He created it to be lived in and enjoyed. These verses take us back to the Genesis account of creation. There we read that God created the world to be good, orderly, and beautiful. Since we are created in God's image and given responsibility over His creation, we, too, should create works of goodness, orderliness, and beauty. Tragically, though, by our selfish exploitation of the earth's resources, we create evil instead of good, chaos instead of order, and ugliness instead of beauty. God may have created the world to be lived in, but we have made large sections of it unlivable by cutting down forests, filling the oceans with trash and microplastics, strip-mining for minerals, polluting the rivers and streams. This not only works against our best interests, but it violates God's purposes for His creation.

The prophet closes this part of his message and our scripture lesson by underlining the uniqueness of God. While those who pray to an idol pray to a god that cannot save, God invites everyone to come to Him and be saved (45:20–22). Furthermore, the prophet is absolutely confident that God would do whatever He promised, and he saw the time when every knee everywhere would bow before Him and every tongue would swear allegiance to Him (45:23–25). This would be a time when people of many nations would join with Israel to seek righteousness and strength from the Lord, and any who did not would be judged.

Throughout this entire lesson, we see the marvelous truth that God is not oblivious to either the affairs of history or the future. In fact, history is His-story—God's story, and He is still very active in it. And He will continue to be active in everything that concerns His people in the twenty-first century and beyond. Our destiny is not shaped by a god made with human hands or by human invention. Our destiny is in the hands of the God who created our universe and who is in charge of it.

Almighty God, thank You that my destiny is cradled in Your hands of love. My life is not one big accident—I am part of Your eternal plan. AMEN.

Fear not, for I am with you; be not dismayed, for I am your God; I will strengthen you, I will help you, I will uphold you with my righteous right hand.

—Isaiah 41:10 (ESV)

"Rockin-Rollercoaster? What's that?" I ask my older sister, Mara, as we stare at the taunting guitar-shaped red-and-black sign.

"No clue, but we've gotta do it. We may never have another chance!" Mara answers, speed-walking toward the line. "Let's go!"

We knew what to expect from the other roller coasters, but this one's new, and all indoors, so we can't see what we're up against. Not a good combo, but we'll be fine, we're together.

Still hesitant, we get in line with Dad. He's fearless, more focused on taking pictures than on the so-scary-they-had-to-keep-it-inside roller coaster. It's our turn. Dad gets on first, sitting with a stranger so Mara and I can sit together. Instead of getting on, though, we examine the other vacationers in line.

One of them is just a kid, maybe nine years old. Mara and I make eye contact, clearly thinking the same thing: *If he can do this, a teenager and a 22-year-old can too!* Then he starts crying. Instantly employees appear and escort him and his family through previously invisible doors. We're pushed forward.

I'm in front, so I slide onto the rigid-but-soft plastic seats first. Looking over, I see Mara eyeing the exit. She's gonna leave me! I can't leave, though, that'd be too embarrassing, but I'm too scared to ride alone. Should I cry?

Before I can decide, Mara sits beside me, and we're locked in. I'm not alone. My eyes are closed for most of the ride, but I'm OK. Someone I trust is with me.

—Rachel Thompson

Notes

Notes

LESSON 6: ISAIAH 46:1–53:12

The Servant of the Lord

Almighty God, teach me how to be Your servant, to obediently do what You call me to. Amen.

Impotent Idols and the Omnipotent God (46:1–13)

God's Redemptive Plan

One of the most significant archaeological discoveries of all time was Napoleon's chance finding of the Rosetta Stone in AD 1799. It happened when he led his army into Egypt. One of his engineers was digging in the sand to erect barricades against the enemy. His digging turned up an unusual stone. It contained a proclamation written in three different languages in honor of Pharoah Ptolemy V, dated 196 BC.

The first two were Egyptian languages written in hieroglyphics, which up to that time had never been deciphered. However, the third language was Greek, a language with which linguists had long been familiar. The Greek section of the Rosetta Stone provided the key to two previously unknown Egyptian languages and unlocked the vast treasures of ancient Egyptian literature.

This scripture lesson focuses on God's redemptive message and furnishes us with the key to understanding why God called Israel to be His covenant people. It was through them that His message of redemption was to go out to all of the people and nations of the world.

There is no other part of the Bible where the oneness and uniqueness of Israel's God are more emphasized than in the last chapters of the book of Isaiah. The theological term used to describe this oneness and uniqueness is monotheism. And the logical sequel to monotheism is missions, for if there is only one God, then it follows that He is the God of *all* nations and will be satisfied only when they all pledge allegiance to Him. It was Israel's mission to bear witness to Him throughout all the world. This was the reason Israel was especially chosen by God and was the key to its existence.

In a similar way, the new Israel, the church of our Lord Jesus Christ, exists for the purpose of bearing witness to Him. Like Israel of old, Christians are called to be "a kingdom of priests, and an holy nation" (Exodus 19:6, KJV). Furthermore, Christians are to be "a light to the nations" (Isaiah 42:6, ESV), doing everything possible to move toward that day when every knee shall bow and every tongue shall swear allegiance to the one true God (Isaiah 45:23).

A humorous story is told of a monk who had to preach a practice sermon as part of his theological training. He was unusually timid, and when he stood up before the other monks, his mind went blank. Finally all he could say was "Do you know what I am going to say?" When all those present began to shake their heads, he said, "Neither do I know," whereupon he dismissed the group.

A second opportunity was given the monk a week later, but though he had spent long hours in preparation, his mind again went blank. After another painful silence he asked, "Do you know what I am going to say?" This time those sitting in the audience nodded their heads, and he said, "If you already know what I am going to say, then there is no need for me to say it," and again he dismissed them.

A third and final opportunity was given the timid monk after another week had passed, but all his efforts were again in vain. The third time his mind went blank when he faced his audience. Again he asked the inevitable question, "Do you know what I am going to say?" This time the audience was thoroughly confused; some shook their heads, while others nodded. This time the monk said, "I see that some of you know what I am going to say, and some of you don't know what I am going to say. If those of you who know will tell those who don't know, then everyone will know."

The point is made: if those of us who know the redeeming power of God's love will tell those who don't know, then everyone will know. This is our task, and this is our glorious privilege.

The Folly of Idolatry

In this part of our lesson the prophet returns once more to the familiar theme of the folly of worshipping idols. He is making a deliberate attack upon the religion of the Babylonians as he heaps scorn and ridicule upon their chief gods, Bel and Nebo (46:1). Bel, meaning "lord," was sometimes used as a title for Marduk (also written Merodach), the patron god of the capital city of Babylon (see Jeremiah 50:2). Nebo, the son of Marduk, was the god of writing and bookkeeping, of wisdom and oratory, of the arts and sciences. He corresponded to the Greek god Hermes and to the Latin god Mercury. It is interesting to note that certain Babylonian personal names are compounded with Nebo, the most familiar being Nebuchadnezzar, meaning "O Nebo, protect the heir (king)."

Gods That Must Be Carried

The prophet describes the state of panic that will follow the fall of Babylon. Its citizens will frantically try to save their gods by loading them on the backs of animals. However, the tired and overloaded animals can barely carry the load (46:1). Since the pagan gods can do nothing to ease the burden of the refugees, they become a part of the baggage that is carried off into captivity (46:2). Idol gods become a load and not a lift. It makes all the difference in the world whether our religion is something we have to carry or something that carries us.

The God Who Carries His People

The God of Israel relates to His people in an entirely different way from the false gods of Babylon. The prophet reminds the people that their God has been with them—carried them—since before they were born, and will continue to do so until they reach old age (46:3–4). Perhaps the analogy used here is that of a mother carrying her child. This promise means that God will never stop carrying His people, and these words take on added significance when seen in their historical setting. They were spoken to disheartened exile-refugees who were convinced that the Lord had forsaken them (see 49:14). But now the prophet assures them that the One who made them will continue to care for them as long as they live.

We gather from the warning in these verses that the Israelites still needed to be cautioned against the dangers of idolatry. The religion of the Babylonians had apparently attracted some of them. Some of the Israelites had come to believe that Bel and Nebo were stronger gods than the Lord. Such being the case, why shouldn't they adopt the religion of their conquerors?

God's prophet waged a relentless battle against this kind of thinking. Not only were the gods of Babylon deadweight to their followers (46:1–2), but they were also a useless waste of precious resources (46:6). And when their help was needed, they were unable to respond to prayer or to deliver anyone from distress (46:7).

The God Who Acts

The prophet next reminds the people of Israel that the Lord's superiority to idols had been demonstrated by the mighty acts He had performed for them since the beginning of their history. The people are urged to "remember this . . . remember the former things of old"—to remember God's mighty acts (46:8–9, KJV). As they recalled their miraculous exodus from Egypt, the care God extended to them during their migrant years in the wilderness, and their safe passage across the Jordan River into the land of promise, they should have had ample reason to be encouraged and full of hope. As they reflected on the glory of their past, the majestic affirmation, "I am God, and there is none like me" (46:9, KJV), must indeed have fired their imaginations!

Next, though, came an important word: God was more than just the God of the past; He was also the God of the future, the designer of "things that are not yet done" (46:10, KJV). These future plans have especially to do with Cyrus, who is described here as "a bird of prey from the east, the man of my counsel from a far country" (46:11, ESV). But there is more: everything the Lord intends to accomplish through Cyrus will happen.

Then comes the parting shot as the prophet urges the "stubborn-hearted" people to listen (46:12, NIV). In spite of their rebellious spirit, the Lord assures them of His deliverance and of His salvation (46:13) and that "it is not far away" (NIV). This seems to indicate that this part of our scripture lesson should perhaps be dated shortly before Cyrus's conquest of Babylon in 539 BC.

Babylon's Day of Reckoning (47:1–15)

The founder of the Neo-Babylonian Empire was Nabopolassar, the father of Nebuchadnezzar. While this empire soon attained splendid heights, it was exceedingly short-lived, lasting only from 626 BC to 539 BC. Nebuchadnezzar reigned during a major part of this time (605–562 BC) and was responsible for most of the splendor of Babylon. He rebuilt the temple of Marduk, famous for its great eastern gate, which remained shut all year long except during the New Year Festival in the spring. At that time, it was opened and the images of Marduk and Nebo passed through it to be carried in procession through the streets of Babylon (see 45:20).

Nebuchadnezzar also built up the defenses of Babylon. An enormous double wall was built around the city. The outer wall was made of sun-baked brick and measured 25 feet in thickness and more than 17 miles in length. The inner wall was 23 feet thick. Access to the city was provided by eight gates, the most famous being the Ishtar gate, an arched passageway 15 feet wide and 30 feet high, flanked on either side by massive square towers. The great Ishtar gate was covered with blue enameled bricks decorated with rows of brightly colored bulls and dragons. The city's great ziggurat, together with the royal palace and its hanging gardens, made it a legend in the ancient world. This is reflected in Nebuchadnezzar's own words: "Is not this the great Babylon I have built as the royal residence, by my mighty power and for the glory of my majesty?" (Daniel 4:30, NIV).

Nebuchadnezzar conquered and destroyed Jerusalem in 587 BC. At that time the Lord's Temple was also destroyed and its sacred vessels carried to Babylon to be placed in the temple of Marduk (see 2 Kings 25:13–15; Daniel 1:2). The indignities heaped upon the Jews caused them to hate the Babylonians as much as any other people who had ever oppressed them. This helps to explain the enthusiasm with which the prophet predicts the downfall of this hated enemy (47:1–15; see Psalm 137:1–9).

From the Throne to the Dust Heap

The prophet in highly colorful language warns that like some proud virgin queen, Babylon will soon be taken off its throne and made to sit in the dust (47:1). It will no longer "be called tender and delicate" (NASB). Carrying the analogy further, the prophet sees the "virgin daughter of Babylon" (verse 1,

NASB) reduced to the level of a slave and stripped of all signifiers of royalty (47:2–3).

The prophet's confidence in the ultimate downfall of Babylon is rooted in his faith in Israel's God, whom he refers to as "our Redeemer, the LORD of hosts . . . the Holy One of Israel" (47:4, KJV). At the time in which the prophet spoke, it probably seemed presumptuous to believe that a God whose Temple had been destroyed and whose people had been taken captive into exile would be delivering a threat to such a mighty nation as Babylon.

A Nation without Compassion

Next we learn that the Lord's anger is directed against Babylon—not because it destroyed Judah and Jerusalem, for it was He who gave it power to do so (47:6; see also 42:24–25), but because the Babylonians were needlessly cruel to the weak and the helpless exiles (47:5–6). Cruelty is never condoned by God, whether it is practiced by an individual or by a group. Sometimes we allow ourselves to do things as part of a group that we would never consider doing as an individual. We must never forget, however, that we incur corporate guilt whenever we do so.

Our corporate sins include the neglect of the poor and homeless in our society, the oppression of women and minority groups, rampant militarism, a judicial system and tax brackets that favor the wealthy, and a nationalism that sometimes places the authority of the state or an individual leader above that of God. These are some of the "nation's sins" for which we all need to repent and earnestly seek God's forgiveness.

Pride and False Security

The prophet tells us now that Babylon also is condemned for its pride and arrogance (47:7–11). Instead of seeing themselves as an instrument in the hands of the Lord, the Babylonians boast that their dominion will last forever (47:7). They are quoted as saying, "I am, and none else beside me" (47:8, 10, KJV), using terminology that is appropriate only when applied to God (see 43:11; 45:5, 6, 21; 46:9). It is the ultimate blasphemy whenever nations or individuals begin to talk and act as if they are God.

The prophet then makes it clear that Babylon's day of judgment is coming soon. Again, employing picture language, Babylon is compared to a childless widow and a people with a false sense of security whose doom and desolation is certain (47:9–11).

False Saviors

With ill-disguised sarcasm, the writer suggests to the people of Babylon that as trouble approaches, they call for help from sorcerers (47:12), astrologers (47:13), and magicians (47:15)—those who turn to the stars and the planets for wisdom. Actually, astrology had its beginnings in Mesopotamia around roughly 3000 BC. The prophet knew the Babylonians put their faith in the movement of the heavenly bodies within the twelve signs of the zodiac and not in God.

Babylon began to decline soon after the death of Nebuchadnezzar, and it never regained its lost splendor. It was finally destroyed by Alexander the Great when he overran the Persian Empire in 330 BC. Once destroyed, it was never rebuilt. The abandoned mound that was once the most splendid city of the world can be seen today, approximately 60 miles south of Baghdad, despite decades of war and political turmoil in Iraq. The ruins were designated a UNESCO World Heritage site in 2019. The silent ruins of Babylon are a witness to the temporal nature of even the mightiest works of human hands. They also are witness to the fate that will eventually overtake all oppressor nations. "The grass withers and the flowers fall, but the word of our God endures forever" (40:8, NIV).

The Tragedy of Wasted Opportunity (48:1–22)

This part of our scripture lesson consists of a mixture of messages of condemnation and messages of hope and consolation. The prophet addresses his words to the exiles just before their departure from Babylon, as evidenced by his stirring call for them to leave the city (48:20). After this chapter there are no further references to Cyrus or to Babylon in the rest of the book of Isaiah. It is as if all memories of them were left behind as the returning exiles faced Jerusalem and the new life awaiting them there.

An Obstinate People

The prophet now focuses his attention on the Jewish exiles and vehemently lashes out at them for being obstinate (48:4), idolatrous (48:5), and deaf (48:8). The root of their problem was their refusal to listen to and obey the word of the Lord (48:8; see also 48:18; 6:9–10; 42:18–20; Amos 2:11–12), but they kept up the appearance of being a religious people. They still swore allegiance to the Lord and professed to believe in Him (48:1). In short, they had all the outward marks of true believers.

However, the prophet saw through this outward show of piousness and accused them of doing these things insincerely and hypocritically (48:1). They might fool others, and even themselves, but they could not fool God.

We need to be reminded that God's purposes in history have always been realized through imperfect human beings. Throughout this part of the book of Isaiah there is a twofold characterization of the nation of Israel. It is portrayed both as the servant of God and as a rebel against God. This twofold characterization is certainly valid based on what we know of the history of Israel. Israel not only gave birth to the prophets, but it also persecuted them. It not only followed God in the wilderness but also turned away from Him in Canaan. The Bible is unsparing in its disclosure of Israel's stubborn disobedience, while at the same time it testifies to its unique calling and destiny. Even in the darkest hours of Israel's history, there were still those who remained faithful to the Lord.

God still chooses to work through weak, frail human beings to accomplish His purposes for the world. This truth should save us from despair on the one hand and from an attitude of self-righteousness on the other. Why should we doubt that God can work today through imperfect persons like us, or through imperfect churches and imperfect denominations? On the other hand, why should we try to take credit for our accomplishments, as if we could have done them without the help of God? Such an attitude of pride and self-sufficiency should have no place among Christians.

Lord of Creation and History

Once again the Jewish exiles are told that the same Lord who laid the foundation of the earth and stretched out the heavens (48:13) is working to shape the future of His people through Cyrus (48:14–15). Even though Cyrus is not mentioned by name here, it is clear that the prophet had him in mind (45:1–4). When the prophet said, "The LORD loves him" (verse 14, NASB), it meant the Lord had chosen Cyrus to accomplish His purposes with the Babylonians, who are also spoken of here as the Chaldeans (48:14–15).

Here in this prophecy the Lord appeals to the Israelites to come to Him and to listen to His words (48:16), reminding them that from the beginning He has not spoken to them in secret but openly (see 45:19; Deuteronomy 30:11–14). The point being made here is God's will has been made clear for everyone who wishes to follow it.

Wasted Opportunity

There is heart-tugging pathos in the Lord's words now as He says, "Oh that you had paid attention to my commandments! Then your peace would have been like a river, and your righteousness like the waves of the sea" (48:18, ESV). "If only" and "what might have been" are among the saddest words in any language. They speak eloquently of lost and wasted opportunity. The story of Israel's long history as the people of God is largely the story of wasted opportunity.

God had such wonderful plans for them, but they preferred to go their own way. And in so doing they forfeited the blessings He had prepared for them. Among the things they lost were God's gifts of peace, righteousness, descendants, and a name that would never be forgotten (48:18–19). If the people of Israel had only known the high cost of their disobedience, they could have been spared the terrible loss of so much.

Once again, though, we can't help but shout, "Amazing grace!" Yes, Israel's history, like our own, is one of wasted opportunities and disobedience. And even now with the promise of deliverance from foreign oppression and the anticipation of "returning home," they were being willful and stubborn. Yet God didn't write them off; He didn't desert them. How thankful we are that God was patient with them and that He is with us!

Summons to Leave Babylon

Now comes the grand announcement, "Go out from Babylon! Flee from the Chaldeans! Declare with the sound of joyful shouting, proclaim this, send it out to the end of the earth; say, 'The LORD has redeemed His servant Jacob'" (48:20, NASB). They were free at last, free to leave Babylon and begin the long trip west to Jerusalem.

Then, lest any of the Jews be reluctant to undertake the difficult journey back to Jerusalem, the prophet reminded them of how the Lord took care of their forefathers when they came out of Egypt. In their journey across the desert and wilderness of the Sinai Peninsula, they did not suffer thirst, for the Lord gave them water from the rock (48:21; see Exodus 17:6;

1 Corinthians 10:4). After all, if the Lord looked after them during the long trip from Egypt to Canaan, He could be counted on to see them through from Babylon to Jerusalem!

This part of our scripture lesson closes with this warning: "'There is no peace,' says the LORD, 'for the wicked'" (48:22, NIV). Earlier the prophet had mentioned those whose peace had been forfeited because of their refusal to obey God's commandments (48:18). The new commandment now given to the exiles was that they were to leave Babylon and begin the journey homeward (48:20).

Apparently, though, some of them were reluctant to leave the security of Babylon and risk the uncertainties of an unknown future back in Palestine. Josephus, the early Jewish historian, reports that many of them chose to remain in Babylon, "being unwilling to leave their possessions" (*Jewish Antiquities, Volume IV: Book XI.* Translated by Ralph Marcus. Loeb Classical Library 326. Harvard University Press, 1937). But the prophet warned them that they would never find peace because they valued security more than obedience to the will of God. They had grown soft in Babylon and were willing to settle for easy success rather than risk great failure. It is still true that those who live by this philosophy never know the deeper meaning of peace.

From Despair to Celebration (49:1–26)

Chapters 49–55 of Isaiah are a kind of interlude between the first command for the exiles to leave Babylon (48:20) and their final departure (see 55:12–13). In this interlude much is said about the mission of the servant of the Lord and the spiritual redemption of the people of Israel, as well as the people of other nations. In fact, three of the four so-called Servant Songs are found in this section of Isaiah. They occur in 49:1–6; 50:4–9; and 52:13–53:12. The other Servant Song is found in 42:1–4.

These Servant Songs are all written in poetry, and they talk about an unnamed person who is given a special mission as the servant of the Lord. His mission is to restore the disobedient Israelites to the Lord and also to be a light to pagan Gentile nations to lead them to faith in the Lord.

Was the servant welcomed by those to whom he was sent? It becomes increasingly clear as we work our way through the four Servant Songs that the answer is no. On the contrary, opposition to him seems to have built up to the point that he was put on trial and then executed. His death, however, was not the end of his career, since he continued to make intercession for sinners, and his sacrificial death provided atonement for transgressors.

Who was the servant of whom the prophet spoke in these four songs? Some have identified him with the prophet, others with the entire nation of Israelites, and others with the Messiah. It is this last interpretation that is adopted by the writers of the New Testament (see Acts 8:26–35).

The Servant Addresses the Nations

The difficulty of identifying the servant of the Lord is nowhere more apparent than in this second Servant Song (49:1–6). On the one hand, the servant is addressed as Israel (49:3), and many of the statements made here about him are repeated elsewhere about Israel. Both are called from birth (49:1, 5; see 44:2, 24). Both are entrusted with the word of the Lord (49:2; see 44:26; 51:16; 59:21). Both are hidden in the shadow of the Lord's hand (49:2; see 51:16). Both are designated to be the Lord's servant (49:2; see 41:9; 43:10; 44:21). Both are charged with the responsibility of glorifying God (49:3; see 43:7; 44:23; 46:13). Both suffer times of discouragement and despair (49:4; see 42:19; 49:14). And finally, both are given a mission to the nations of the world (49:6; see 42:6). It would be irresponsible to deny that the prophet at times designates Israel as the servant of the Lord.

At the same time, certain obstacles seem to stand in the way of this interpretation. For example, the servant is charged with the responsibility of raising up the tribes of Jacob and restoring the preserved of Israel (49:6). But how could Israel perform these tasks on its own behalf? How could Israel restore the preserved of Israel?

It seems, therefore, that we must make room for another interpretation even if the two must be held in tension. After all, the tension is inherent in the verses themselves. For while the servant coexists with Israel, and is even addressed as Israel, he is at the same time distinct from Israel and called to perform a ministry to Israel. The paradox involved here must have been just as obvious to the prophet as it is to us, and therefore fully intentional. Furthermore, the figure of the servant never lost its paradoxical character across the centuries, for when the time of its fulfillment came, it was fulfilled in Jesus Christ *and* in His church. Just as Jesus was the Suffering

Servant of the Lord, so are we called to be God's servants. We are to take up the cross and follow Jesus's steps.

Of this we can be sure: our service for the Lord involves serving our fellow human beings.

The Spiritual Deliverer

In this second Servant Song the servant calls upon distant lands to listen to him, for the Lord has called him (49:1) and made his mouth "like a sharp sword" (49:2, ESV; see 50:4). This means that the weapon with which he does battle is the word of the Lord, an indication of the prophetic nature of his mission (see Deuteronomy18:18; Jeremiah 1:9; 5:14).

Twice it is said that the Lord hides the servant (49:2), which means that he is always under the Lord's care and protection (see Psalms 17:8; 27:5; Jeremiah 36:26). Then the initial task assigned to the servant is related to the restoration of Israel (49:5). As Cyrus was called to be a political deliverer, so the servant was called to be a spiritual deliverer. As is so often the case, spiritual restoration proved far more difficult to achieve than political restoration. The servant met with resistance from the very people whom he had been called to serve, and he soon became discouraged (49:4). His discouragement is very much like that of Jeremiah when he was caught in similar circumstances (see Jeremiah 9:2; 15:18). This reminds us, too, of Jesus's experience in the Garden of Gethsemane (see Luke 22:39–46).

God responded to the discouragement of the servant by expanding the scope of his ministry. "I will also make You a light of the nations so that My salvation may reach to the end of the earth" (49:6, NASB). His ministry was to all people everywhere.

Hope for the Downhearted

As the prophet continues, we realize that the Jews are still in exile (49:7–11). The people are described as being hated and still imprisoned, and their land, Jerusalem and Judah, still lies desolate. The years of exile have been a bitter experience.

All this, however, was about to end, and their release from captivity is described as if it were a second exodus. This time, however, it is the Lord Himself and not Moses who cares for them like a shepherd, providing pasture along the way (49:9) and leading them to springs of water (49:10). He also prepares a highway in the desert for their safety and comfort (49:11; see also 35:8–10; 40:3–4; 55:12–13).

The prophet suggests that not only will the Babylonian exiles return to Jerusalem but Jewish refugees from other places will also find their way back (49:12). With the coming of that realization, the prophet breaks out in song (49:13; see also 12:1–6; 52:9). And this song reminds us of the one the Israelites sang after their earlier deliverance at the Red Sea (see Exodus 15: 1–18; Revelation 15:2–4). The religion of the Bible has always been a singing religion. This explains why hymns and worship songs are such a vital part of our worship services.

The Restoration of Zion

Zion, pictured here as a woman, speaks out in despair because she believes the Lord has forsaken and forgotten her (49:14–21). It is difficult to know whether Zion stands for the remnant of Jews left in Jerusalem or for the exiled community in Babylon. The lament expressed here would fit equally well with either group. It was a time of great despair for both segments of the nation (see Lamentations 1:4–5, 17; 2:10, 13; 5:1–22; Psalm 137; Ezekiel 37:11–14).

The Lord responds to Zion's cry of despair with one of the tenderest expressions of divine love to be found anywhere in the Bible. He tells the despondent people that His love for them is greater than the strongest form of human love, greater than a mother's love for her nursing child. Furthermore, He assures them that under no circumstance would He ever forget them (49:15–16).

These tender, emotive words, along with those found in Psalm 23, Psalm 103, and Hosea 11, belie the common belief that the God of the Old Testament is only a God of harsh justice, while the God of the New Testament is a God of love. In reality, neither testament presents nor describes an unloving God. His strong love, which conquers all human sin and resistance, serves as the cord that binds both the Old and the New Testament together.

The remaining verses in this section (49:17–21) look ahead to the miraculous rebuilding and repopulation of Zion. The prophet expected Jerusalem to be restored in the near future. And the once desolate city will welcome home refugees from all over the world. In fact, we're told the city will be crowded out.

The Future Greatness of Zion

In this short prophecy the Isaiah writer looks into the near future and foresees the Jewish exiles actually making their return to Jerusalem with the help of their captors (49:22–26). The prophet's listeners, still imprisoned in Babylon, must have been skeptical that this really could ever happen, for they asked in utter disbelief, "Can the prey be taken from the mighty, or the captives of a tyrant be rescued?" (49:24, ESV). It is clear that they doubted that any power could ever deliver them from the hands of the Babylonians. The Lord's response echoes and answers their skeptical questions as assurance that He personally will intervene: "Even the captives of the mighty shall be taken, and the prey of the tyrant be rescued for I will contend with those who contend with you, and I will save your children" (49:25, ESV). The graphic wording of verse 26 makes us shudder, but it is likely descriptive of the self-destructiveness of war, whether in the sixth century BC or in our present century.

Faithless Servants and the Faithful Servant (50:1–11)

The Lord's Faithful Servant

A contrast is now drawn between the disobedience of the people of Israel (50:1–2) and the obedience of the Lord's servant in this the third of the Servant Songs (50:4–9). First, in speaking of the servant, we're told that the Lord has given him a trained tongue (50:4) and an attentive ear (50:4–5). In other words, the servant knows how to listen and how to speak. Through his words he is able to comfort and encourage those who are weary.

Next, the theme of persecution makes its first appearance in the Servant Songs (50:6), prompting some interpreters to refer to this third Servant Song as "the Gethsemane of the servant." This theme is brought to a climax in the last Servant Song when the servant suffers a violent death at the hands of wicked people (see 53:7–9).

What is emphasized here is the voluntary nature of the servant's suffering. He willingly exposes himself to humiliation (50:6). This attitude alone is enough to distinguish the servant from the nation of Israel, for they never learned to suffer willingly or in silence.

The song ends with the servant's confident affirmation of victory (50:7–9). He is so confident of vindication that he challenges his accuser to bring charges against him (50:8). He knows the Lord God will come to his defense and that he never will be condemned (50:9). This strong affirmation of faith reminds us of similar words spoken by Paul: "If God be for us, who can be against us?" (Romans 8:31, KJV).

The Consequences of Sin

Utilizing vivid picture language, the prophet now seems to be inviting those who still walk in darkness to fear the Lord and to obey the voice of His servant (50:10). It is implied that their situation would be reversed if only they would trust in the Lord and take refuge in their God.

On the other hand, those who continue to disobey God will inevitably suffer the consequences of their sin. The Apostle Paul presented the contrast in these words: "For the wages of sin is death, but the gracious gift of God is eternal life in Christ Jesus our Lord" (Romans 6:23, NASB).

Assurance of Salvation (51:1–52:12)

Encouragement to the Fainthearted

The prophet never forgets that his call is to comfort captive Israel (see 40:1–2). Apparently, despite the assurance they had, the exiles had lost heart because of their small numbers. They wondered how they could possibly escape from the mighty forces that held them captive in Babylon (see 49:24), and even if by some miracle they did manage to escape, how they could ever make it back to Jerusalem and rebuild the city. It was rather a staggering agenda.

In response to their doubts, the Lord tells them to remember Abraham and Sarah (51:1–2). When their father Abraham and their mother Sarah had no children, God had called them and blessed them and in a miraculous way gave them an heir. If God did that for Abraham and Sarah, certainly He could act boldly for them! But what they needed was the same quality of faith that Abraham had. The fact that the exiles were about to leave the same land where Abraham and Sarah had first been called makes this word of encouragement even more meaningful.

Once again the people of Israel are reminded to remember the past in order to obtain hope for the future. And that future is pictured as a time of unparalleled joy, a time when the waste places of Jerusalem would be restored like the garden of Eden (51:3). The prophet foresaw the day of the Lord drawing near, the day when the Lord's salvation would be revealed (51:4–5).

Next, we have that contrast between the fragile nature of the creation and the enduring nature of God's salvation (51:6).

Equally fragile and perishable would be the efforts of the pagan nations to frighten and terrorize the people of God (51:7). Those who opposed the Lord's people would disappear from the scene, and in this world of change and decay only God's salvation would last from generation to generation (51:7–8).

The command to the exiles to remember Abraham and Sarah should remind us that a vital part of our relationship to God is memory. We all need to be reminded of our roots. We are heirs of a rich stream of tradition that began hundreds of years before Christ and stretches to us in the twenty-first century AD. It is through remembering that we relive the past and draw strength for the present and the future. Memory plays a vital role in our worship together as the family of God. As we take Communion, we remember the atoning death of our Lord Jesus Christ. And by our remembering, we participate in His body and blood (see 1 Corinthians 10:16). In a spiritual sense, we relive the Crucifixion and each of us is enabled to say, "I *was* there when they crucified my Lord!" Remembering makes us participants in the events of our past.

Memory also ought to play a vital part in our private devotion. Through memory we recall those high moments of the past when God seemed especially close to us. Many of us know that our lives have never been the same since He reached down and touched us.

The Christian philosopher, scientist, and mathematician Blaise Pascal had an encounter with God that completely changed his life. He never forgot that experience. After he died, a handwritten account of this event was found stitched inside the lining of his coat. It read, in part:

The year of grace 1654
Monday 23rd November
From about ten at night to half past twelve.
God of Abraham, God of Isaac, God of Jacob,
Not of philosophers and wisemen.
Certainly, joy certainly!
Awareness, peace, joy!
God of Jesus Christ!

It isn't enough, of course, for us to draw strength and inspiration from past experiences alone, however wonderful they may have been. A Christian who knows God only from the past and not from the present is most unfortunate. There is always the need for us to keep our experiences with God up to date. This is why the prophet both appeals to the exiles to remember the past so as to draw strength from it (51:1–2) and also cautions them against the danger of always living in the past (43:18–19). Some people spend so much time talking about "the good old days" that they miss seeing what God is doing in the present.

A Prayer for Help

One of the characteristics of this part of our scripture lesson is the large number of repeated commands and repetitions, such as "Awake, awake . . . !" (51:9), "Awake, awake!" (51:17), "Awake, awake . . . !" (52:1), and "Depart, depart . . . !" (52:11, NIV).

The first "Awake, awake!" (51:9) is Israel's urgent call to God. It is their response to the prophet's exhortation to look to the past and take heart (see 51:1–2). Next, we read that the people plead for God to repeat the mighty works of salvation

He performed in past generations (51:9). Obviously, they have in mind His mighty acts at the time of the exodus out of Egypt (51:9–10). If God would just repeat the miracle of the exodus for the Babylonian exiles, they would return to Jerusalem with singing, joy, and gladness (51:11).

We sense an unusual degree of tenderness in God's response to Israel's appeal for a fresh revelation of His power. The repetition of "I, even I" at the beginning of verse 12 is in response to their repeated call to Him (51:9). God urges them to stop being afraid of other humans, who after all are no more enduring than grass (51:12; see 40:6–8). Fearing other people could only make the people of Israel take their eyes off of God and cause them to forget that the One who created the heavens and the earth also had power to still the fury of the oppressor (51:13). The exiles were naturally anxious to be set free, fearful that they might yet die in their prison (51:14). But at the same time, they needed to remember that He who once divided the sea was still their Lord, and they were His people (51:15–16).

A Bitter Cup

The repeated command, "Awake, awake! Rise up," is addressed to Jerusalem (51:17, NIV). The following verses give a vivid description of the desolate condition of the city at that time. It is compared to a woman staggering about in a drunken stupor who holds a large vessel in her hand that is called the cup of the Lord's wrath (51:17). Jerusalem has had to drink it down to the dregs (51:17), an indication of the severity of its punishment (see 40:2). Then, continuing the picture, as she staggers about in her drunken stupor, none of her sons are able to take her by the hand or help her walk (51:18). They, too, are drunk with the wrath of the Lord and have passed out in the streets (51:20).

Next, God breaks in upon this scene to make a pledge to those who have been forced to drink from the bitter cup (51:21). He pledges to plead their cause and to take from their hands the cup of His fury and place it in the hands of those who have so cruelly and mercilessly oppressed them (51:22–23). This can only mean that Babylon's day of judgment is drawing near (see 47:1–15).

Redeemed without Money

The prophet now directs our attention to Jerusalem: "Awake, awake" (52:1, NASB). And then, in the same verse, he tells the city to "clothe yourself with your beautiful garments" (NASB). These symbolize both strength and holiness. Jerusalem once more will become the holy city, from which the uncircumcised and the unclean will be forever excluded (52:1).

The prophet next appeals to the city of Jerusalem to accept the fact that it is free at last (52:2). The city has in fact been redeemed (52:3). A new day has arrived.

An Exhilarating Climax

This next prophecy provides an exhilarating climax to this part of Isaiah. In his imagination the prophet sees a runner approaching Jerusalem from the north (52:7), from the direction of Babylon. As the messenger draws near the devastated city, he shouts out the glad tidings, "Your God reigns!" (NIV).

The watchmen stationed on the walls of the city catch the sound of his words and sing out their joy (52:8). Before long the entire city is alive with song, like some mighty chorus (52:9). And well might they sing, for the Lord is leading the captives home and all of the earth has seen His great salvation (52:10).

The scene next shifts back to Babylon as we come to the end of this section. There an emancipation proclamation has been issued to the captives. They have received their marching orders at last. They are told to leave Babylon in another of the repeated commands, "Depart ye, depart ye, go ye out" (52:11, KJV). Then special instructions are given to those who bear the "vessels of the LORD" (52:11, KJV). These are most likely the Temple vessels that Nebuchadnezzar removed from Jerusalem and carried to Babylon (see 2 Chronicles 36:18). But when Cyrus conquered Babylon, he permitted the exiles to return these vessels to Jerusalem (see Ezra 1:7–11).

Those participating in the exodus from Babylon would not have to go out in haste as their ancestors had done when they left Egypt (52:12; see Exodus 12:11, 33, 37–39). Rather, they would make a peaceful march across the desert with the Lord keeping watch over them (52:12). The care with which God would guide them on their journey back to Jerusalem is one of the dominant themes throughout chapters 40–55 (see 40:11; 41:17–20; 42:15–16; 43:2; 49:8–10; 51:11; 55:12–13).

The Suffering and Triumph of the Servant (52:13–53:12)

We come now to the fourth and final Servant Song, and it deals with the suffering and triumph of the servant of the Lord. Here the servant is definitely treated as an individual, and sharp contrasts are drawn between his behavior and that of the Israelite nation as a whole. Cyrus had provided political redemption for the people of Israel; the servant through his vicarious suffering and death would provide spiritual redemption.

Jesus deliberately modeled His ministry after the pattern laid down in the Servant Songs, especially this one. He saw Himself as one who was sent to minister to others and to lay down His life for them. He refused to become a political Messiah, like Cyrus (see 45:1), but chose instead to become a suffering Messiah, after the pattern of the servant. This conscious decision influenced not only His death and resurrection but also His entire ministry.

The disciples of Jesus and other early Christians had difficulty at first in comprehending this. If they had not had the Servant Songs to instruct them, they might never have understood why the One who was the object of their messianic hopes had to be crucified. Proof that they depended so heavily upon the fourth Servant Song to explain Jesus's suffering and death is found in the fact that portions of this song are quoted in all four Gospels, as well as in Acts, Romans, Philippians, Hebrews, and 1 Peter. If for some reason the entire song were to be lost from the Old Testament, it could be almost completely reconstructed from the New Testament quotations. Nowhere in the Old Testament do we come so near the Cross of Jesus as here.

This song is composed of five stanzas, each of which is three verses in length. The following outline is suggested:

1. From humiliation to exaltation (52:13–15)
2. The servant's unlikely beginning (53:1–3)

3. The servant's vicarious suffering (53:4–6)
4. The servant's sacrificial death (53:7–9)
5. The servant's ultimate triumph (53:10–12)

From Humiliation to Exaltation

We are first given a summary statement of the servant's rise from humiliation to exaltation (52:13–15). The speaker here is the Lord Himself. He tells how the servant rises to heights of glory (52:13), in spite of his appearance, which is so marred by suffering (52:14). His rise from humiliation to exaltation will be so unexpected that he will startle the nations (perhaps a better rendering than "sprinkle," used in most English translations), and kings will be speechless because of what they see (52:15).

The Servant's Unlikely Beginning

The opening question, "Who has believed our report?" (53:1, NASB) is worded so as to receive a negative response. It was asked either by the Gentile kings referred to in chapter 52, verse 15, or by the Jews themselves, who express astonishment that such an unlikely person should have had such an unusual career.

But God's ways are not our ways, and this is never more apparent than in the choice of those who will be His ministers and proclaim His Word. He chose the Israelites when they were just a motley crew of enslaved people building the storehouses for the pharaoh of Egypt. God chose Moses and Jeremiah over their protests of unworthiness. He took two lowly shepherds, David and Amos, and made one a king and the other a prophet. Jesus chose His disciples from among tax collectors and fishermen. Paul wrote that God deliberately chooses the weak and the despised as His ministers, in order that no human being might boast in His presence (see 1 Corinthians 3:26–29).

The prophet attributes all kinds of misfortunes to the servant (53:2–3). He is described as a stunted plant, struggling to survive in hostile dry ground. His physical appearance is so grotesque that others turn away to avoid looking at him. Verse 3 has often been interpreted to mean that he was afflicted with the loathsome disease of leprosy, a disease that caused others to hide their faces in fear and revulsion. It is understandable, therefore, that he should be spoken of as "despised and rejected" by humankind, "a man of suffering, and familiar with pain" (53:3, NIV).

The Servant's Vicarious Suffering

It has been said that the Old Testament reflects three levels of understanding regarding the meaning of suffering. At the first level, all sufferers are regarded as being sinners. This is the level of understanding reflected, for example, in the speeches of Job's friends, who insisted, despite Job's repeated denials, that he was suffering because of some sin he had committed. At the second level, some sufferers, such as Job and Jeremiah, are acknowledged to be saints. Their suffering remains an enigma both for them and for others. At the third level, some sufferers are regarded as saviors, because they willingly suffer for the sake of others. Their suffering has redemptive value because of its vicarious nature.

The servant's suffering fits this third category. The speakers can only say in amazement, "He has borne our griefs and carried our sorrows" (53:4, ESV). He "was pierced for our transgressions, he was crushed for our iniquities; the punishment that brought us peace was on him, and by his wounds we are healed" (53:5, NIV). This all comes to a climax when the speakers freely confess that they had all gone astray like sheep, each turning to his own way, but that the Lord had laid upon His servant the blame that should have been theirs (53:6).

A more modern example of vicarious suffering involved Maksymilian Kolbe, a Polish Catholic priest, imprisoned by the Nazis at Auschwitz. He became a martyr when he saw another prisoner, a Polish army sergeant named Franciszek Gajowniczek, being led to the gas chambers. Father Kolbe was standing nearby when he heard the condemned man cry out, "Oh, my poor wife and children!" Kolbe immediately stepped up to the officer in charge and asked if he might take Gajowniczek's place, and to everyone's surprise the officer agreed. Gajowniczek escaped execution and survived the war because Kolbe took his place, and he lived to the age of 93. He later spoke of this experience in these words, "I had been sentenced to death and someone had offered his life for mine of his own free will."

This, of course, is what Jesus has done for all of us.

The Servant's Sacrificial Death

The death of the servant is presented as the sacrifice of the innocent for the guilty (53:7–9). And yet it is a sacrifice that occurs outside the Temple and its sacrificial system. The victim is an innocent person, and his sacrifice makes all other sacrifices unnecessary.

This must not be interpreted to mean that his sacrifice works automatically to remove sin. It is effective only for those who make it the means of their approach to God. It is effective only for those who confess that He "was pierced for our transgressions; he was crushed for our iniquities" (Isaiah 53:5, ESV). Such a confession is impossible apart from repentance. But when that confession is made from the heart, it always leads to forgiveness.

A deliberate contrast is drawn between the crowd of sinners and the lone servant (53:6–7). The crowd confesses, "All we *like sheep* have gone astray" (53:6, KJV; italics added for emphasis), but he, *like a sheep*, is led "to the slaughter" (53:7, KJV). But still he did not open his mouth either to complain or to condemn. In the servant we have a unique example of the innocent suffering in silence.

The Servant's Ultimate Triumph

The most surprising thing about the story of the servant is that it does not end with his death. We learn first of all that his suffering and death were within the will and purpose of the Lord (53:10). The Lord willed that His servant should be put to death, not because of any anger toward the servant but because of His love for sinners. The servant's death, therefore, was not the hopeless end of a tragic life but rather the crowning event of that life, at least from God's standpoint. Death was the servant's greatest achievement, the achievement by which sinners could be restored to favor with God. The servant thus fulfilled his mission through his sacrificial death, but the results extended far beyond his death.

This song may have referred originally to some unnamed Israelite who would suffer and die on behalf of his contemporaries. If so, it is impossible to find anyone in Old Testament times who even comes close to fulfilling this prophecy. When Christ came, however, this promise was transposed to a higher key and found its perfect fulfillment in Him. He was the Suffering Servant of the Lord in a way no other person has ever been.

Lessons for Today

As we come to the end of this important part of the book of Isaiah, we might look at some of its lessons for our day.

First, God's ultimate purpose for His people will succeed despite opposition from a hostile world. This truth is emphasized in Psalm 76:10: "Surely your wrath against mankind brings you praise, and the survivors of your wrath are restrained" (NIV).

Second, God may use whomever He chooses in accomplishing His purposes. He often seems to find His servants in the most unlikely places. Who would ever have supposed that a ruler like Cyrus, who neither professed nor demonstrated faith in the one true God, would be chosen to set the Jewish exiles free and make possible the rebuilding of Jerusalem? Who could have predicted that Saul the persecutor would become Paul the apostle?

Third, while God may sometimes work through unbelievers today, the church is still His chief instrument for the working out of His purpose in the world. There is no way we can shift this responsibility to others. Just as the nation of Israel was called to be a witness and a servant of God, so are we.

Faithfulness in witnessing and in serving is the hallmark of true believers.

Fourth, there is only one God to whom the people of all nations may look for salvation. We live in a time when many people believe that all faiths are much the same and that one's religion is merely a matter of personal preference. The prophets of Israel cried out in protest against those who thought like this. They, too, lived in a world filled with a variety of gods, but they believed that only one God could save. They faithfully proclaimed this God to all the nations. And we are to follow their example!

Gracious Lord, how grateful I am to know You—the only, almighty, all-knowing God who has shown me the way to find You. May I forever praise You for Your glory and grace. AMEN.

We all, like sheep, have gone astray, each of us has turned to our own way; and the LORD has laid on him the iniquity of us all.

—Isaiah 53:6 (NIV)

When my husband and I decided to replace our kitchen countertops, my father offered to save us hundreds of dollars by cutting down our current split-level countertop and moving the electrical outlets himself. A few days later, after the countertop was removed, I explored the progress. The cabinets were in a curved island, so the dead space between the individual sections was exposed. I looked inside, and that's when I saw it—Isaiah 53:6 written in pencil on the back side of the drywall. Right away, I recognized the verse and knew who had written it. It was my father's favorite verse. The entire Gospel, squished into one sentence, pointing the reader to Jesus.

I've watched my dad manage construction projects my whole life. He's built swing sets, churches, patios, birdhouses, buildings, and a cross so tall that airplane pilots navigate around it. I've also watched my dad grow in his walk with Jesus. He's never taken for granted the grace that he, an admitted sinner, has received through Christ. He knows it's unlikely someone will find his hidden messages, but he still leaves Isaiah 53:6 behind when he builds. It's hope for the future. An answer to a question not yet asked. Salvation for sinners not yet born. If just one person sees the reference, looks up the verse, and follows their curiosity to find Jesus, it'll be worth it.

Dad, I saw your hidden message. But more so, I see your love for Jesus.

—Emily E. Ryan

Notes

Notes

LESSON 7: ISAIAH 54:1–59:21

The Ecstasy and the Agony of Freedom

Gracious Lord, help me to be faithful to my Christian commitment, even when the glamour begins to fade, even when the loaves and fishes run out, even when it gets hard. AMEN.

Chapters 54 and 55 of the book of Isaiah describe the outward circumstances of the Jewish exiles and the emotions they experienced as they awaited the word that they could actually begin the trip from Babylon to Jerusalem and Judah. The only word that would adequately describe their response to this long-anticipated event would be *ecstasy*.

However, as we shall see, once they made the arduous journey back to Jerusalem, the glamour began to fade. Problems closed in on them from every side—some of which they had not anticipated. The returning exiles, few in number, were totally at the mercy of their Persian overlords. And their hostile neighbors used pressure to delay their rebuilding of the Temple. Jerusalem's wall still lay in ruins and would not be rebuilt until more than a century had passed. Disuse and neglect had ruined the productivity of their soil, resulting in crop failure and famine. It didn't take long for the exiles to discover that in addition to the ecstasy of freedom, there was also the agony of resentment. The story of how they responded to the problems they encountered is found in chapters 56–66.

The Glorious Heritage of the Servants of the Lord (54:1–17)

The title for this part of our lesson is borrowed from verse 17. Our scripture lesson gives us a colorful description of the glorious future awaiting the exiles upon their return to Jerusalem. Chapter 54 is written in the second person feminine gender as if it was written to a deserted wife—"forsaken and grieved in spirit" (54:6, KJV). Jerusalem, of course, is that deserted wife.

A Population Explosion

Looking into the future, the prophet first speaks of the unexpected increase in Jerusalem's population (54:1–3). It was unexpected because the city's current condition could be compared to that of a barren woman (54:1), the same term as that used in the book of Genesis to describe Sarah, the barren wife of Abraham (11:30). Then, building on the comparison, Jerusalem is described as "desolate," as translated in most Bible versions, perhaps meaning that she felt forsaken by the Lord (see 50:1).

But then we have the picture of the barren and desolate woman becoming the parent and protector of many children. The writer compares her to a desert nomad who would need to enlarge her tent by lengthening its cords and strengthening the stakes in order to make room for her enlarged family (54:2). And next, the prophet sees the people of Jerusalem spilling out across the countryside and settling in other desolate cities of Judah and even in certain foreign territory (54:3). These verses are a useful commentary on the earlier statement of the prophet that said the Lord created the heavens and the earth not to become a chaos but to be inhabited (45:18). He is always the God of order, not of disorder. It is we who create disorder and barrenness.

On May 31, 1792, William Carey, a British Baptist minister who supplemented his meager income by cobbling shoes, preached a world-changing sermon before a gathering of his fellow ministers at Kettering, England. He took as his text the words of Isaiah 54:2, "Enlarge the place of thy tent, and let them stretch forth the curtains of thine habitations: spare not, lengthen thy cords, and strengthen thy stakes" (KJV).

Carey's sermon was organized around two main points: (1) We should expect great things from God; and (2) we should attempt great things for God. In his sermon he made a passionate appeal for his listeners to accept responsibility for the worldwide mission of the church. Under the inspiration of his sermon, the Baptist Missionary Society was formed on October 2, 1792, an event that many regard as the initial step in the launching of the modern missionary movement. A year later, Carey himself was appointed by the newly formed missionary society to begin what proved to be a long and distinguished career as a missionary to Serampore, India. It was this prophetic word from Isaiah that gave a unique missionary shape to modern church history.

The Return of the Prodigal Wife

The prophet now moves into the metaphor of the estranged wife as a woman betrothed in her youth but rejected by her husband-to-be (54:6). We next see that the husband who had separated from her and the bridegroom who had rejected her was none other than the Lord Himself (54:5, 7). And the separation and the rejection refer to the years spent in exile in Babylon (see Hosea 3:4).

But now the time of separation was about to end. Her time of shame and reproach would soon be forgotten (54:4), and she would be reunited to her Husband and Redeemer, who was none other than her Maker, the Lord of hosts, the Holy One of Israel, the God of all the earth (54:5).

The time of separation is explained briefly as having been a necessary judgment from God—"For a brief moment I abandoned you," but that is immediately contrasted by the words "but with deep compassion I will bring you back" (54:7, NIV) and "with everlasting kindness I will have compassion on you" (54:8, NIV). The Bible teaches that God's judgment is always a "strange work" or "unusual task" (Isaiah 28:21, NIV and NASB, respectively). His first and greatest desire is always to bless us (see Ezekiel 18:23; 2 Peter 3:9).

Everlasting Peace and Security

The prophet then compares the exile to the flood in the days of Noah. At that time, when the water had gone down, God declared that the earth would never again be destroyed by floodwaters (54:9; see Genesis 9:11). Now, as their time of exile was almost over, God said that He would never again be angry with Israel nor rebuke her (54:9). These words are understood to mean that God would never again judge the people of Israel with that kind of oppression. This promise must have been welcome news to the returning exiles.

Just as God established His covenant with Noah after the flood (see Genesis 9:8–17), so now He promises to reestablish His covenant with the restored exiles (54:10). He declared that His promise was more secure and more durable than the mountains and the hills (54:10; see also 51:6; Mark 13:31). And his kindness would never depart from them, neither would His covenant of peace be revoked.

The prophet's words "O afflicted one, storm-tossed and not comforted" in verse 11 (ESV) underline the fact that the Jews were still in Babylon; their release had not yet occurred. But the Isaiah writer now goes on to give a preview of what they could expect to happen once they arrived back in Jerusalem and Judah.

This is what the prophet saw. The city itself would be rebuilt with the most precious gems (54:11b–12), a description of beauty and grandeur that reminds us of John's vision of the New Jerusalem in Revelation 21:9–27. The people would be taught by the Lord Himself, and they would be free from oppression—they would be at peace (54:13). Once again, Jerusalem would be a city of righteousness (54:14), a goal referred to over and over again in the book of Isaiah (see 1:26; 28:16–17; 32:16–17; 33:5; 48:18).

Next, the prophet seems to say that while enemy forces may storm and even take Jerusalem at some future time, it won't be by His judgment, and no one will succeed in destroying the

Lord's people. No weapon fashioned against the Lord's people would prosper, and any charge brought against them would result in the condemnation of the one bringing it (54:17). This was the heritage the Lord had provided for His people (54:17). Paul expressed a confidence similar to this when he wrote, "What shall we then say to these things? If God be for us, who can be against us?" (Romans 8:31, KJV).

Invitation to Freedom (55:1–13)

This part of Isaiah contains God's invitation to those who had survived the long years of exile and had witnessed Cyrus's conquest of Babylon. Freedom was now in their grasp, but they must reach out and seize it. However, not all of the Jews were eager to leave Babylon, even when given the opportunity to do so. Some were reluctant to exchange the security they knew in Babylon for the insecurity that awaited them in Palestine.

This accounts for the urgency expressed by the prophet as he speaks to the exiles now. He became like a recruiting officer in the Lord's army, trying to fill out the ranks for the return to Palestine. He employed both the stick and the carrot method, combining threat with promise, as he tried to recruit the reluctant exiles to accompany him on the journey back home.

A Crucial Choice

The Isaiah writer at this point offers the exiles a crucial choice. They could either partake of the nourishing food and drink that the Lord offered free of charge, or they could spend their money for that which neither nourished nor satisfied (55:1–2). This meant that they could either return to Palestine to participate in the rich future God had in store for them, or else they could remain in Babylon and forget about going home. But the prophet found it inconceivable that anyone would choose the latter option.

Next, God's plans for Israel's future were set forth (55:3–5). God wanted His people to listen to Him in order that they might live, and in order that the everlasting covenant made with David (2 Samuel 7; 23) might be transferred to them (55:3). But Israel's selection as God's special people was not merely to privilege; it also involved heavy responsibilities. The people of Israel were charged with the responsibility of witnessing to the sovereignty of the Lord to other nations of the world. They were the instrument in God's hands for a worldwide mission.

One of the biggest hazards facing Christians is that of "underliving." We somehow feel that we have too much to lose to be fully committed to God. So we remain marginal Christians all our lives, never quite sure about where to place our priorities. Like the Jewish exiles, we would like to help rebuild "Jerusalem," but the pull of "Babylon" is too strong. However, anyone who thinks he or she has too much to lose to be fully committed to God hasn't even begun to understand the blessings of living a life committed to the Lord.

A Call to Repentance

The next stanza in this poem carries an urgent appeal to the exiles to turn their backs on their own evil thoughts and ways and turn to the Lord for mercy and pardon. These marvelous words have challenged people for centuries, "Seek the Lord while He may be found; call upon Him while He is near. Let the wicked abandon his way, and the unrighteous person his thoughts; and let him return to the Lord, and He will have compassion on him, and to our God, for He will abundantly pardon" (Isaiah 55:6–7, NASB).

Then, if by chance any of the Jews should protest their innocence or deny their need for repentance, the prophet reminded them of the great gulf separating their thoughts and ways from the thoughts and ways of God (55:8–9). This reminder is needed in every generation, for there is a perennial tendency among people—especially among religious people—to confuse their own thoughts and ways with those of God and to adopt an attitude of moral superiority and arrogance. Nothing alienates people from God more quickly than this attitude on the part of those who claim to be His people.

God's Dependable Word

The prophet's next words seem to have been addressed to certain scoffers among the exiles who had expressed doubts about the reliability of God's Word (55:10–11). The same prophet who himself had earlier been reassured of the reliability of God's Word (see 40:8) now sets out to reassure others. He urges those doubters to put God to the test, for in doing so, they would discover that His promised blessings were as certain as the harvest that had been watered by the rains and snows from heaven. God's Word could always be relied on just as surely as the cycle of the seasons.

Homeward Bound

In a final attempt to lure the exiles to leave Babylon, the prophet painted an idealistic picture of the journey homeward (55:12–13). He described the journey across the desert as if it would be a continuous outdoor celebration, or a victory march from some distant field of battle.

As Isaiah described it, this new exodus for God's people would be celebrated by all of nature—the mountains and hills would break out into singing, and the trees of the field would keep time by clapping their hands (55:12). And as they marched along through the desert, it would be transformed into a victory memorial garden filled with stately trees and flowering shrubs.

Summarizing the message of this part of Isaiah, we see that it was of vital importance for the exiles to obey God's call and leave Babylon. The prophet's appeal for them to do this was based on four great truths:

1. God alone can satisfy the deep needs of the human spirit (55:1–2).
2. Israel's true destiny was to serve as a witness to the nations and to call them to acknowledge the sovereignty of God (55:3–5).
3. Israel's opportunity to respond had to be seized at once, or it might be lost forever (55:6–9).
4. God is faithful, and His promises never fail (55:10–11).

And each of these eternal truths applies as much to Christians today as to those Jews in Babylon.

The Difficulties of Beginning Again (56:1–59:21)

When the exiles finally arrived in Jerusalem, they discovered that they could not simply turn the clock back to 587 BC and experience life the way it was before the Babylonians came. Their years in Babylon had created a different set of problems, and they soon became painfully aware of this.

One of the most urgent problems had to do with postponed promises. They had been told that Jerusalem and the Temple were to be restored (see 44:28), that there would be a tremendous increase in the city's population (see 49:19–21; 54:1–3), that the wealth of the surrounding nations would be theirs (see 45:14), and that kings and queens would volunteer to serve them in even the most menial tasks (see 49:22–23).

It would be a gross understatement to say that the fulfillment of these promises did not meet their expectations. For example, they lacked the resources in workers and materials to rebuild Jerusalem and the Temple. Crop failure and famine were commonplace occurrences (see Haggai 1:6, 9–11; 2:16–17). Tribute had to be paid to Persia and supplies furnished to the soldiers stationed in the land (see Nehemiah 5:15). Instead of being free of foreign oppression, they were destined to remain under Persian control for more than two more centuries.

According to the wisdom writer, "Hope deferred makes the heart sick" (Proverbs 13:12, NIV). When the future the exiles had hoped for failed to materialize, they began to doubt that the Lord loved them (see Malachi 1:2), or that there was any benefit to be derived from serving Him (see Malachi 3:14).

The remaining chapters of the book of Isaiah are addressed to those who were wrestling with the problems of resettlement in Palestine. The focus of attention, therefore, shifts from Babylon to Jerusalem. There is no further reference to Cyrus or to the servant of the Lord. On the other hand, there are numerous references to the "servants of the Lord," but this becomes a technical term used to describe true believers within the Jerusalem community.

The prophet's task now was to give guidance to the people of Jerusalem and Judah in a time of change and uncertainty. He must explain the delay in the fulfillment of their hope and rekindle their confidence in the Lord and in the ultimate fulfillment of His promises. The prophet's success in accomplishing his task is attested by the fact that the faith of Israel was able to survive during the difficult years that followed.

We've all probably experienced those uneventful waiting periods in our lives when we are forced to wrestle with the problems similar to those Jerusalem Jews faced. These are the times when God's promises seem either to have failed or to have been postponed indefinitely. These are the times when our mouthful of idealism meets the grim reality of the real world, when our dreams have to be scaled back to meet that reality, and when spiritual fatigue sets in and we are tempted to give up.

These last chapters of Isaiah have a great deal to say to those of us who have sometimes felt like saying, "What's the use? I'm tired of beating my head against a stone wall. I can't take it anymore!" They remind us that God is still at work and in charge, even in the waiting periods of life. At such times we are reminded that cynicism and despair come from our having lost touch with God. And finally, we are reminded that God has promised not to give up until He has created new heavens and a new earth. So we, too, must not give up until His promises have been fulfilled.

Inclusion or Exclusion?

During their years of exile in Babylon, some of the Jewish young men had been made eunuchs by their Babylonian captors. This was so they could be trusted with positions of responsibility in the royal palace. Some of these eunuchs were among those who returned to Jerusalem. Apparently, too, certain foreigners, perhaps encouraged by the prophet himself, had decided to accompany the returning exiles to Jerusalem.

The presence of eunuchs and foreigners in their midst created problems for the Jerusalem community (56:1–8). There was apparently a division of opinion as to whether or not they should have citizenship rights or be allowed to participate in Temple worship. On one side were the strict legalists who opposed the inclusion of foreigners or physically deformed Jews in the worship life of the community. They could even claim scriptural support for their religious exclusiveness (see Deuteronomy 23:1–8; Ezekiel 44:9).

But there was another group that championed the rights of foreigners and eunuchs to full participation in the Lord's worship. The prophet obviously belonged to this second group, because he taught that no person should be denied access to the Temple or acceptance in the community of Israel because of racial or physical considerations. The only demands placed upon them were that they should keep the Sabbath, avoid evil, do good, and uphold the covenant (56:2, 4).

Eunuchs who satisfied these demands were promised acceptance and were assured that God would look beyond their physical condition and give them a place of honor among His people and "a name better than that of sons and daughters" (56:5, NASB; see also verses 3–4). Also, foreigners who had become proselytes to the Jewish religion were welcomed to the Temple and allowed to offer their sacrifices (56:6–7). In one of the most inclusive statements found in the Scriptures, the Lord declares that His house should be called a house of prayer for all people (56:7; see Mark 11:17). But that isn't all. The assurance is given to all people everywhere that the invitation is open to them to become a part of God's covenant people (56:8; see 49:5–6; John 10:16).

The problems the prophet dealt with here are of perennial concern to us as the people of God. Two questions demand attention: Upon what basis are people to be admitted to the life and ministry of the church? Should we be inclusive or exclusive? The moment we exclude others on the basis of such things as gender, color, or class, we are in danger of denying the universality of the gospel and of refusing to accept as brothers and sisters those whom God has already accepted as His sons and daughters.

A story is told of a college faculty member who grew up in a rural community where there was strong prejudice against all foreigners. One Sunday a family of people who had immigrated to the United States and had recently arrived in town came to worship at one of the town's thriving churches. The church members were sharply divided over the question of the appropriate response to the newcomers. Some wanted to extend a warm welcome to them, but others wanted to inform them that they were not welcome. Unfortunately, the latter group was in the majority, and after a hastily called business session, they sent a delegation to inform the family that they must worship elsewhere.

From that moment on the church began to decline, until finally it was forced to close its doors. The empty building stood as a monument to a dead church, a church that had forgotten that there are no limits to God's love, except as we try to place limits upon it. God still wants His house to be a house of prayer for all people (56:7).

Blind Watchmen

No book of the Bible devotes so much attention to the problem of spiritual blindness as does the book of Isaiah (see 6:10; 42:18–19; 59:10). In our scripture lesson now, the prophet launches a strong attack on Israel's leaders—blind watchmen and self-indulgent shepherds (56:9–12). In the Old Testament, the prophets were symbolically described as watchmen (see 21:6–12; 52:8; 62:6; Ezekiel 3:16–21), while kings were described as shepherds (see 2 Samuel 5:2; 1 Kings 22:17; Ezekiel 34:1–10). Tragically, Israel's prophets had become undependable and corrupt watchmen, and Israel's shepherds were guilty of leading a self-centered existence. They failed to understand the needs of the people, because "they have all turned to their own way, each to his own gain, one and all" (56:11, ESV). The prophet sees them as living from one drinking party to the next, and trying to make each one more lavish than the one that preceded it (56:12).

This was indeed a description of what happened after the Jews got resettled in Jerusalem. And it shows how difficult it was to root out sin from Israel, even after they had suffered the hardships of exile. Sometimes we wonder if punishment ever succeeds in improving character.

A Return to Idolatry

In addition, we now discover that after the returning Jews got resettled in their homeland, their old battle against idolatry had to be confronted again (57:1–13). Corrupt and weak leadership by prophets and rulers (56:10–12) had opened the way for societal and religious safeguards to be weakened, allowing pagan tendencies that had long been dormant to emerge.

Also, the people of Israel are charged with other gross sins: the violent removal of righteous persons from the community (57:1), open mockery against God (57:4), child sacrifice (57:5), and cult prostitution (57:7–9).

Next comes the sordid picture of people so trapped by sin that they were unable to break away from it, even though they were tired of it. They suffered from what has been called the atrophy of the will. This means that disobedience brings about a growing inability to obey. A life of sin never provides complete satisfaction, but it offers just enough enticement to keep people from abandoning it.

God's Mercy and Judgment

The prophet continues now with further evidence of the decline in the spiritual level of the Jewish community after their return to Jerusalem (57:14–21). Despite the consequences they had endured, they continued to slide deeper into sin (57:17). Their life could be compared to an abandoned roadway, left in such a state of disrepair and so covered with debris that it was no longer passable. Consequently, the Lord called for them to rebuild their lives and to clear them of every obstacle that might hinder their return to Him (57:14; see 40:3–5; 62:10–12).

Why were the people to seek God? The remainder of this part of our scripture lesson gives reasons why the people should abandon their sinful ways and follow God. First, they were to seek God because He dwelt not only in the highest heaven but also with those of a contrite and humble spirit (57:15; see 66:2; Psalms 34:18; 113:4–9; Proverbs 16:18–19; Matthew 5:3–5; 11:28–29). Second, they were to seek Him because the time of His wrath had ended, and He was now ready to forgive their sins and to revive their spirits (57:16–18). Finally, they were to seek and follow God because only in Him could they find healing and peace (57:19–21).

What Does the Lord Require?

What does the Lord want from us, and what do we consider to be essential to a right relationship with Him? Our answers to these questions determine the character of our religion and our behavior. This is why so many writers of Scripture struggled with these questions and tried to come up with meaningful answers (see Psalms 15; 24:3–5; Amos 5:21–23; Micah 6:6–8).

Apparently, the Jerusalem Jews who had returned from Babylon placed fasting near the top of their list of God's requirements (58:1–14). The purpose of their fasting was to make God more favorably disposed toward them in their times of distress (see 1 Samuel 7:6; 2 Samuel 12:16; 2 Chronicles 20:2–3; Joel 1:14). The only fast prescribed in the Pentateuch is that related to the Day of Atonement (see Leviticus 16:29; Numbers 29:7; Acts 27:9). Four more fast days were added during the exile in Babylon to commemorate the fall of Jerusalem and other disasters that followed soon after this (see Zechariah 7:3, 5; 8:19).

It is likely that the prophet preached this particular sermon that makes up our scripture lesson now to the people who had gathered to observe one of these fasts. Most likely it was on the Day of Atonement. There is evidence elsewhere that in the post-exilic period the practice of fasting came to be regarded as an acceptable substitute for true repentance and ethical living (see Jeremiah 14:10–12; Zechariah 7:1–10; 8:19; Malachi 3:13–14). It is always dangerous when people define their duty toward God in terms of abstinence rather than action. There is always the danger of doing a religious exercise like fasting out of a selfish and ulterior motive. It may be done simply for the emotional satisfaction it provides. Or it may be done to gain the approval and commendation of others. Jesus vigorously condemned fasting in order to impress other people (see Matthew 6:16–18).

An Exercise in Futility

Our scripture lesson teaches that fasting may also become a form of self-deception. The prophet was told to make the people understand the seriousness of their transgressions and sins (58:1). But all the while the people imagined that they were fully meeting God's demands. After all, they were going through the motions—they sought Him daily, delighted to know His ways, asked Him for righteous judgments, and took pleasure in approaching Him (58:2). They bore a striking resemblance to the Pharisee of whom Jesus spoke, who stood in the Temple and prayed this prayer: "God, I thank you that I am not like other people—robbers, evildoers, adulterers—or even like this tax collector. I fast twice a week and give a tenth of all I get" (Luke 18:11–12, NIV).

The returned exiles even complained to God that their fasting had not paid off. They asked, "Why have we fasted and You do not see? Why have we humbled ourselves and You do not notice?" (58:3, NASB). Their questions indicated that their motives for serving God were selfish and mercenary. They thought that because they had regularly attended the Temple and fasted and prayed, God was obligated to bless them. According to their calculations, God distributed rewards and punishments strictly based on merit, and they judged that their merits obligated Him to reward them.

But the prophet told them that their fasting was an exercise in futility because it left them indifferent to the needs of others. Abstaining from food only made them more irritable and more likely to strike out at others (58:4). The Lord made it clear that their self-inflicted punishment was not pleasing to Him, and that it didn't increase the likelihood that their prayers would be answered (58:4b–5). The "fast" that God wanted was a genuine concern for the needs of others. It was striking out against all forms of oppression (58:6), being concerned to provide food for the hungry, for the homeless and the naked (58:7; see also Matthew 25:34–40). If they did these things, God would be pleased with them.

If you do this, the prophet said, you will be amply rewarded. The rewards included light, healing, response to prayer, good health, unfailing strength, and a continuing influence for good in the life of the community (58:8–12). The prophet who spoke these words had a passion for social justice that was as strong as that of any of the pre-exilic prophets. His words challenge us to reexamine what we consider to be essential to a right relationship to God in our day and time. We are always in danger of substituting the *forms* of religion for its substance.

When Promises Are Postponed

As we've already noted, the people who returned from Babylon had expected an immediate fulfillment of God's promises. And when that didn't happen, they complained bitterly and resumed their sinful practices. In our lesson now they are complaining that the Lord's hand is shortened so He could not save, and His ear so dull He could not hear (59:1–8). To have the hand shortened meant to lose the power and strength to act effectively (see 50:2; Numbers 11:23). To have a heavy ear was to be dull of hearing or intentionally deaf (see 6:10; 42:19; 43:8). The people were accusing the Lord of being unwilling to hear their cries for help and unable to do anything to remedy their situation. This means that they accepted no personal blame for their predicament but blamed everything on the Lord.

The prophet immediately tried to set the record straight by informing them that it was their iniquities and sins that had alienated them from God and caused a postponement of His promises (59:2). Then he goes into detail with a colorful description of their sins. "For your hands are stained with blood, your fingers with guilt. Your lips have spoken falsely, and your tongue mutters wicked things. No one calls for justice; no one pleads a case with integrity. They rely on empty arguments, they utter lies; they conceive trouble and give birth to evil" (Isaiah 59:3–4, NIV). And then the prophet adds, "Their feet rush into sin" (59:7, NIV).

These were devastating accusations in the light of all that the people had been through in Babylon. They, more than anyone else, should have understood the importance of dealing justly with others. They, more than anyone else, should have learned to respect basic human rights. Justice often suffers at the hands of those who themselves have previously been the victims of injustice. There is never any excuse for injustice, but it is even less excusable when practiced by those who should know better.

The prophet then goes on to use the metaphor of hatching vipers' eggs (59:5) to describe the deadly influence of lives like theirs. If someone ate one of the eggs, he or she would die. On the other hand, if they tried to destroy one of the eggs by crushing it, a viper would come out of it. This illustrates the truth that sin has a way of multiplying that often defies explanation.

According to the prophet, there was no way for persons like these to achieve their own righteousness before God.

For them to try to do so would be like weaving a spider's web and then trying to make a garment out of it (59:5–6). And to be covered with such a garment would certainly not hide a person's sin and iniquity. Human attempts to cover sin have always proved to be inadequate (see 64:6; Genesis 3:7, 21). Only God can provide a covering that is adequate (see 61:10).

The bitter results of a life of injustice, sin, and iniquity are mentioned next. These include being condemned to walk on a road of ruin and destruction (59:7), and never being able to find peace (59:8), without which life itself is not worth living (see 26:3; 32:17; 48:18, 22; 55:12).

Israel's Confession and God's Response

The prophet next offers a prayer of confession on behalf of the people (59:9–15). Note the wide range of words he uses to describe their sins: transgressions (59:12), sins (59:12), iniquities (59:12), inciting revolt and oppression (59:13), turning away from God (59:13), speaking oppression and revolt (59:13), uttering . . . lying words (59:13), and preventing justice, righteousness, truth, and uprightness (59:14).

These were devastating accusations, and it is no wonder the people were plunged into feelings of hopelessness. "Therefore justice is far from us, and righteousness does not overtake us; we hope for light, and behold, darkness, and for brightness, but we walk in gloom" (59:9, ESV). The prophet continues as he speaks of them stumbling and groping as if they were blind and groaning in their despair like dumb animals or birds (59:10–11). He speaks of their consciences being burdened with guilt (59:12–13), and then he adds that justice, truth, and equity were no longer practiced (59:14–15).

The prophet responded to the confession with a promise of salvation (59:15b–21). Of particular significance is the way God is portrayed in these verses:

1. He was not at a distance from His people nor unconcerned about their welfare (59:15).
2. When no one offered to intervene on behalf of His people, God did so Himself (59:16; see also 63:3–5).
3. Although in this description God is pictured as a Warrior, His protective armor is quite unusual—a breastplate of righteousness, a helmet of salvation, "garments of vengeance," and a robe of zeal (59:17; see also Ephesians 6:13–17; 1 Thessalonians 5:8).
4. God's intervention would result in the destruction of His enemies (59:18), while at the same time it would bring honor and glory to His name (59:19).
5. He is the Redeemer to all who repent of their sin and give up their evil ways (59:20).
6. He promised to establish His covenant with them, and to give them His spirit and His words, "from this time forth and forevermore" (59:21, ESV). With this kind of God, the people of Jerusalem and Judah most certainly had every reason to put their trust in Him.

Lessons for Today

Nothing we have studied in Isaiah so far is of greater relevance to us than this lesson. We still wrestle with the same problems that were faced by the people in Jerusalem. The lessons God wanted His people in the Jerusalem community to learn apply equally to us today.

We must never reject as our brothers and sisters those whom God accepts as His sons and daughters. The error of Jonah was that he tried to place a limit on God's love. He failed to realize that God is not the enemy of those we regard as our enemies but that His love and mercy are freely offered to everyone, without regard to characteristics such as nationality, race, gender, or social status.

When the practice of religion becomes an end in itself, it hinders rather than helps our approach to God. A good example of this drawn from biblical times is the practice of fasting. Fasting is a form of self-denial. But self-denial, in and of itself, has no spiritual meaning. The prophet brings this into focus when he insists that going without a meal has no spiritual value unless we share a meal with a hungry person.

Then, too, if we ask, "What must we give up for the Lord?" this prophet's reply would be, "Give up injustice! Give up selfish living! Give up self-indulgence! Give up neglect of the poor, the homeless, the oppressed! Give up pride born of position, race, status, and religion! Give up prejudice and malice toward others! If you do this, your life will be pleasing to the Lord."

A healthy prayer life is one of the sure marks of a healthy Christian. It was God's intention that His Temple be a *house of prayer* for everyone. And there shouldn't be any question about our need for prayer. If God's people had no other reason for coming together except to pray, then that would be reason enough for maintaining a place and time for meeting.

It is interesting to observe the importance the prophet attached to Sabbath observance (58:13–14). He knew that God's people needed a space of calmness at the end of a busy week, a time of festive rest, a time to think of something more important than earning one's livelihood.

Rewards are still promised for faithful service to our Lord, but we should learn to serve without becoming too concerned about what we shall receive in return. The happiest Christians are those who concentrate on helping others and leave the bookkeeping to God. Those who have caught the spirit of Jesus do not speak of their sacrifices or of what they have given up for God. Instead, they focus on their joy in Christian service and the satisfaction they have received. They see their life as a wonderful adventure they wouldn't miss for all the world.

Heavenly Father, thank You for the adventure of serving You! Amen.

"For my thoughts are not your thoughts, neither are your ways my ways," declares the Lord. "As the heavens are higher than the earth, so are my ways higher than your ways and my thoughts than your thoughts."

—Isaiah 55:8–9 (NIV)

My husband was assembling an aluminum storage shed in our backyard. I sat on the grass studying the instructions. After he screwed together several walls, I interrupted. "I think you did that wrong. The dark side is supposed to be on the inside."

Together we puzzled over the drawings and reread the ambiguous directions. My husband patiently agreed to try it my way. He disassembled everything and put the pieces together a new way. I was wrong. The shed was now inside out.

Sometimes I also try to grab the pattern of my life from the hands of the Lord and tell Him what He's doing wrong. His ways seem inside out when they're works in progress. I come up with better plans. Doesn't He want me to step in to explain to my friend what she's doing wrong? Doesn't He want me to tell everyone what I believe are the root problems in my church? Doesn't He want me to stridently defend Him when someone questions my faith?

My way makes sense until the structures I build tumble down.

Instead, God calls me to serve my friend with compassion as she struggles, or to repent when I'm part of the problem in my church, or to listen with love to a person full of doubts. His ways aren't my ways. When I trust that His love and His wisdom provide a better plan, I give Him room to work.

—Sharon Hinck

Notes

Notes

Future Restoration of Zion

Heavenly Father, help me receive the truths You have for me in this lesson and in my life. Amen.

Promise of a New Day (60:1–62:12)

A Light for All Nations

Nowhere is the future glory of Jerusalem depicted in more vivid colors than in this passage (60:1–14). In his mind's eye the prophet imagined Jerusalem flooded with light while all the surrounding landscape lay in darkness (60:2). The imagery in the prophet's description is rich in the colors of the ancient Near East. He sees camel caravans loaded with treasure making their way along the trade routes toward Jerusalem (60:6). And his vision extends to the Mediterranean, where he sees ships loaded with cargo headed for Israel's coast (60:8–9). In the prophet's eyes, Jerusalem and Judah are beehives of activity as the ruined city is rebuilt and refurbished.

The prophet began this oracle with two double imperatives directed to Jerusalem. The first (60:1) told her to arise and shine, because "the glory of the Lord rises upon you" (NIV). The term "the glory of the Lord" first appears in Scripture in the story of the building of the Tabernacle at Mount Sinai (see Exodus 24:15–17). We read twice that after the Tabernacle had been finished, "the glory of the LORD filled the tabernacle" (Exodus 40:34–35, NIV).

Glory is sometimes used in an ordinary sense in the Old Testament—to describe someone's wealth, dignity, and status in the community. But when applied to God, it refers to the revelation of His power and holiness. The glory of the Lord is usually described in the Bible as a bright light or a burning fire that both reveals and conceals God's presence. It reveals enough to confirm the faith of the observers and conceals enough to make them humble and reverent. A normal reaction for someone brought face-to-face with the vision of God's glory is an overpowering sense of sin and unworthiness (see Isaiah 6:1–5).

The prophet's picture here is one of foreign movement toward Jerusalem because of the brilliance of the city's restoration and of the glory of the Lord. It gives us an interesting insight into the missionary strategy of the Old Testament, a strategy that differed somewhat from that of the New Testament. The strategy of the New Testament might be classified as centrifugal, or directed and moving out from the center, which means that Christ's disciples were sent out from Jerusalem into all the world and commanded to make disciples of all the nations (see Matthew 10:5–15; 28:18–20; Acts 1:6–8). In the Old Testament, however, the strategy was more centripetal, or moving toward the center, which means that Jerusalem was to draw foreign people and nations to the city because of its commitment to the Lord and to His covenant. The people of Israel were not sent out to the surrounding countries because they were expected to come to her (see Isaiah 2:2–3; 45:14–15; Zechariah 8:20–23; 14:16–17). Being faithful to God was the

Jerusalem community's first priority; going out with God's message was secondary. One possible takeaway for us today is that if we all were to place more emphasis on truly being the Lord's people and applying His priorities in every part of our lives, we would be much more effective at bringing others to Jesus, either at home or overseas.

The prophet moves on now to further describe the restoration of Jerusalem (60:10–14) to its former glory. The walls and gates are rebuilt, and the Lord's Temple is restored. And people, former enemies as well as friends, would acknowledge that indeed Jerusalem was "The city of the LORD, The Zion of the Holy One of Israel" (60:14, KJV). Many interpreters over the years have seen the fulfillment of this prophecy in the descriptive words in the book of Revelation (21:24–27).

A Vivid Contrast

Now the prophet gives us a vivid before-and-after contrast (60:15–22). While Jerusalem had "been forsaken and hated," the city was destined to be "an object of pride forever, a joy from generation to generation" (60:15, NASB). The city's days of being treated like an orphan would be over, and her wealth would be restored under responsible leadership. Peace and righteousness would govern the city (60:16–18).

The theme of light that was introduced earlier (60:1–3) reappears now (60:19–20). Employing superb poetic imagery, the prophet describes the glory of Jerusalem's exaltation: "The sun shall be no more your light by day, nor for brightness shall the moon give you light; but the LORD will be your everlasting light, and your God will be your glory. Your sun shall no more go down, nor your moon withdraw itself; for the LORD will be your everlasting light, and your days of mourning shall be ended" (ESV).

Tidings of Great Joy

We come now to one of the most frequently quoted proclamations of the prophet (61:1–11). This sermon or prophecy opens with a bold declaration of his calling and intention: "The Spirit of the Sovereign LORD is on me, because the LORD has anointed me to proclaim good news to the poor. He has sent me to bind up the brokenhearted, to proclaim freedom for the captives and release from darkness for the prisoners, to proclaim the year of the LORD's favor and the day of vengeance of our God, to comfort all who mourn" (61:1–2, NIV).

Immediately following Jesus's baptism and temptation experience in the wilderness, He returned to His hometown of Nazareth. There, on the Sabbath day, He went to the synagogue and read these very words from the book of Isaiah (Luke 4:18–19). It is obvious Jesus was drawing a parallel between His mission and that of the prophet. And there is a sense as well in which these words describe the mission of every Christian. Jesus himself indicated as much when He said, "As the Father has sent me, even so I am sending you" (John 20:21, ESV).

If we take seriously the mission outlined here and wholeheartedly devote ourselves to ministering to the needs of the poor, the despised, and the oppressed in our society, we open ourselves to misunderstanding, criticism, and even outright abuse. It is no accident that Luke informs us that Jesus was rejected by those assembled in the house of worship at Nazareth when He read Isaiah 61:1–2 and announced that this would be the model for His own ministry (see Luke 4:14–30). The super-pious crowd in Jesus's day hated Him because He made friends with such lowly persons as tax collectors and sinners (Luke 7:34), and they were really offended when He told them that tax collectors and harlots would enter the kingdom of God ahead of them (Matthew 21:31). There will always be those who want their church to be a closed society with outsiders strictly excluded. If we choose to oppose those people, we must be prepared for the same kind of hostility that Jesus encountered.

The description of the prophet's mission given in these verses says a great deal about the actual condition of those to whom he had been sent to minister. They are described as afflicted, brokenhearted, and bound in prison chains (61:1). While at least some of them had already returned to Jerusalem (61:3), they had not yet been able to repair the walls and buildings, described here as "the desolations of many generations" (61:4, NASB).

These were obviously the same people whose glorious future had been described earlier (chapter 60). This is indicated by a comparison of 60:21 and 61:3. Both of these verses state that the Lord intended to form a community of righteous people who would be called "the planting of the LORD," so that in them He "might be glorified" (KJV). The most likely date for this prophecy seems to be shortly after the first contingent of exiles had returned to Jerusalem, around 538 BC. The verses further suggest that the returning exiles were overwhelmed by the enormous problems that still faced them in restoring and rebuilding the city. They badly needed to hear the message of comfort and encouragement that the prophet spoke to them.

The prophet told them that others would be responsible for the secular side of life—tend their flocks, cultivate their fields, and provide for their material needs (61:5, 6; see 49:23; 60: 10–11, 14, 16). This would make it possible, then, for them to devote themselves to a new spiritual ministry, to being priests and ministers in the service of the Lord (61:6; see Exodus 19:5–6). They were assured they would be amply rewarded for the hardship they would endure (61:7), and God would be faithful to the covenant He had made with them (61:8–9).

In response to "good news" (61:1), the prophet stretches his imagery as he depicts the city of Jerusalem offering God a grand hymn of praise for her salvation and anticipation of complete restoration (61:10–11). The restored city that has arisen from a century of ruin and neglect is compared with the beautiful clothing that would be worn by a bride and groom, emphasizing the mutual joy and delight of God and His redeemed people (61:10; see 49:18; 62:4–5; Hosea 2:19–23; Revelation 21:2). And to convince his listeners of the dependability of God to keep His promises to them, the prophet cites the predictability of nature, "For as the earth brings forth its sprouts, and as a garden causes what is sown in it to sprout up, so the Lord God will cause righteousness and praise to sprout up before all the nations" (61:11, ESV). What a marvelous testimony to the eternal truth that our God can be counted on!

Standing on the Promises of God

Next comes the grand assurance of the prophet that he will neither rest nor keep quiet until the city is restored and the brightness of her salvation can be seen by everyone (62:1). This is one of many passages in the Bible stressing the power of intercessory prayer (see Genesis 18:23–32; Exodus 32:9–14; Isaiah 53:12; Luke 11:5–10; James 5:16–18). The prophet was certain of the glory of Jerusalem's future, and that it would be recognized by Israel's neighbors (62:2). And now he announces that the city will have a new name—they would be a new people (verse 2). Here as elsewhere in the Bible a new name meant a new character and a new personality (see Genesis 17:5; 32:27–28; John 1:42).

Jerusalem's name would no longer be "Forsaken" and "Desolate," but it would now be changed to "Hephzibah" and "Beulah" (62:4). Hephzibah means "my delight is in her." Beulah means "married." The prophet's picture language is expressing the Lord's joy over the restoration of Jerusalem—a joyful "remarriage" between the Lord and His people (62:5). There is no finer statement of the Lord's love for His people in all the Old Testament.

The prophet's next reference to "watchmen upon [the city] walls" (62:6, KJV) is to those charged with the responsibility of maintaining a prayer vigil over the city. He implores them now to take no rest and to give God no rest until Jerusalem was reestablished and made an object of praise in all the earth (62:6–7).

At the same time, the people are told that the Lord will no longer allow foreign predators to rob them of the crops they had planted (62:8). Instead, they would be able to enjoy the fruits of their labor, eating and drinking together and praising the Lord in His holy courts (62:9). This probably referred to the joyous observance of the Feast of Tabernacles, which served as the harvest festival in ancient Israel (see Zechariah 14:16–19).

Chapter 62 ends with the repetition of a theme that runs throughout the latter part of Isaiah. It is the theme of the preparation of a highway in anticipation of the Lord's return to His people and of the people's return to Jerusalem (62:10; see 35:8–10; 40:3–5, 9–11; 59:20–21). Here the highway begins at the gates of Jerusalem and stretches out to the ends of the earth so that exiles, wherever they are, will find their way home.

Chapter 62 also ends with a return to the theme of the new name (62:12; see verses 2, 4). Four new names pointed to the new future awaiting Jerusalem and its people. They were "The Holy People," "The Redeemed of the Lord," "Sought Out," and "A City Not Forsaken" (verse 12, ESV). With names and identity like that, and given to them by the Lord, the people of Jerusalem should never again have questioned who they were.

It is interesting that one of the new titles applied to Jerusalem is a city "Sought Out." This promise has been fulfilled in a way that probably would have surprised the prophet who delivered it. Across the centuries Jerusalem has remained a pilgrimage center for Jews, Christians, and Muslims. Christians have been drawn to it by the thousands. Jerusalem has taken on special significance for them because they remember it as the setting for Jesus's last teaching, His passion,

His death, and His resurrection. It has indeed remained a city "sought out" by millions upon millions of people.

The Doom of Edom (63:1–6)

Bitter Enemies

The struggling post-exilic community at Jerusalem was surrounded by enemy nations. Among the Israelites' bitterest enemies were the Edomites, the only people with whom they shared a common ancestry involving both father and mother. You might recall that Jacob and Esau were the twin sons of Isaac and Rebekah. Few struggles are as bitter as those between brothers, and the Bible dates the struggle between Jacob and Esau to the time when they were both still in their mother's womb. The struggle continued after their birth and came to a climax in Jacob's deceiving his blind father in order to steal Esau's blessing. It is understandable that relations between the Edomites, the descendants of Esau, and the Israelites, the descendants of Jacob, were strained throughout most of their history.

When Jerusalem fell to Babylon in 587 BC, the Edomites aligned with the Babylonian conquerors. The Israelites who tried to flee from Jerusalem were intercepted by the Edomites at the fords of the Jordan and delivered over to the Babylonian pursuers (see Obadiah 10–14). The memory of this act of treachery on the part of the Edomites lingered in the minds of the Israelites long after it was past (see Psalm 137:7; Ezekiel 25:12–14). It is against the background of the hatred between these two nations that this next part of our scripture lesson should be interpreted (63:1–6).

The Mighty Stranger

In his vision the prophet saw a lone figure approaching Jerusalem from the direction of Edom. His steps were like those of a mighty warrior and His garments were stained red, like those worn by someone who had trodden the winepress (63:2). When the prophet asked Him why His garments were red, He replied, "I have trodden the winepress alone. . . . I looked, but there was no one to help, I was appalled that no one gave support; so my own arm achieved salvation for me, and my own wrath sustained me" (63:3, 5, NIV).

The message of the vision was that the Lord had avenged the wrong done to His helpless and defenseless people at the hand of the Edomites. In so doing, He had once again proven Himself to be the friend of the friendless and the executor of justice for the oppressed. This was a message the struggling community at Jerusalem desperately needed to hear.

The underlying truth here is that God does not remain neutral when the weak are oppressed by the strong. There may be no one on earth willing to take up the cause of the weak or defend them, but God remains their champion and their defender. Sometimes He must "tread the winepress alone" as He brings judgment upon the oppressors.

A Prayer of Intercession (63:7–64:12)

The theme of intercession reappears now as the prophet assumed the role of intercessor on behalf of the people of Jerusalem. He identified himself with them to such an extent that his prayer became their prayer.

The prayer begins with a review of God's past acts of mercy toward the Israelites (63:7–14). The rest of his prayer was a confession of national wrongdoing and a plea for forgiveness and deliverance (63:15–64:12). Since Jerusalem and the Temple are described here as still lying in ruins (see 63:18; 64:10–11), this prayer should probably be dated between the first return of the exiles (538 BC) and the rebuilding of the Temple (516 BC). Without question, this was one of the most difficult periods in Israelite history.

Remembering Past Mercies

The prayer of intercession began by referring to the gracious acts of the Lord on behalf of His people in "the days of old" (63:9, 11, ESV). His care had been manifested through His "lovingkindnesses," His "great goodness," and His "compassion" (63:7, AMP). The Hebrew term translated as "lovingkindnesses" (AMP, KJV), "kindnesses" (NIV), "steadfast love" (ESV), and "mercies" (NASB) describes the unwavering, merciful covenant love of the Lord. It is the kind of love that still holds on to us even when we are unworthy.

The single most important event in Israel's history was the exodus out of Egypt. It was preached by the prophets (see Hosea 11:1; Amos 3:1–2; Micah 6:3–5), sung by the poets (see Psalms 77:11–20; 78; 105:26–45; 106; 114; 135; 136), and celebrated in the Passover—the best loved of all Israel's sacrificial feasts. It was through this event that such words as *salvation* and *redemption* first entered the vocabulary of the Old Testament.

The prophet now recalled the events of the exodus as proof of God's love for Israel in the past. He told his listeners how

God became their Savior (63:8), suffered with them in all their affliction, accompanied them with the angel of His presence, redeemed them in His love and pity, and carried them through the past years (63:9). The focus of these words is on the exodus event and the years of the wilderness wanderings.

Despite the Lord's mercies, however, Israel had rebelled against Him and grieved His Holy Spirit (63:10). This probably referred not to a single act of rebellion but to a long series of rebellions stretching from the time of the exodus to the downfall of Jerusalem in 587 BC. Whenever the Israelites rebelled against the Lord, He became "their enemy, and himself fought against them" (63:10, ESV). This, of course, was the situation that led to catastrophes like the Babylonian exile.

Most commentators regard the pronoun "he" at the beginning of verse 11 as referring to Israel. In the midst of their distress, Israel remembered the mighty deeds God had performed in the days of Moses. It was then that Israel cried, "Where is He who brought them up out of the sea with the shepherds of His flock? Where is He who put His Holy Spirit in the midst of them, who caused His glorious arm to go at the right hand of Moses, who divided the waters before them to make for Himself an everlasting name, who led them through the depths? Like the horse in the wilderness, they did not stumble; like the cattle which go down into the valley, the Spirit of the LORD gave them rest. So You led Your people, to make for Yourself a glorious name" (63:11–14, NASB). This question reflected a troubled people who were unable to account for the apparent absence of God in their present time of distress. Now they wanted Him to act again and repeat the deliverance He had accomplished for them centuries before.

Pleading for Present Help

The prophet also prayed for the Lord's help in Israel's present time of need (63:15–64:12). He called upon the Lord not only to look down from heaven (63:15) but also to split the heavens and come down to rescue His people and make His name known to His adversaries (64:1–2). The prophet was asking for a new show of God's power and glory, one that would cause mountains to melt and oceans to boil (64:1–2).

The titles applied to God in this section are significant. He is referred to three times as "our Father" (63:16; 64:8), once as "our Redeemer" (63:16), and once as "our potter" (64:8). These titles emphasize God's love, His redeeming power, and His sovereignty (see 29:16; 45:9; Jeremiah 18:6).

When the prophet asks, "Why, Lord, do you make us wander from your ways and harden our hearts so we do not revere you?" (63:17, NIV), he is reflecting the Old Testament concept that God hardened the hearts of those who rebelled against Him (see Exodus 7:3). A similar thought appeared earlier (64:5): "Behold, you were angry, and we sinned" (ESV). At first sight, these two verses seem to place the responsibility for Israel's sin on God Himself. However, a deeper truth emerges here: the wrath of God sometimes finds expression when a sinful person becomes more deeply involved in evil actions (see Romans 1:18–32). There is a sense in which sin brings its own punishment (64:6). There is nothing more frightening than to be caught in the power of our own sins (64:7).

The prophet next describes the present desolation of Israel in contrast to her more glorious past (63:18–19). The Israelites had once been the holy people of the Lord and had had His sanctuary in their midst (63:18). However, this happy state of affairs lasted a relatively short time before adversaries came in and destroyed the sanctuary (63:18; see 2 Kings 25:8–9). The low morale of the people as they struggled to rebuild Jerusalem and the Temple is reflected in verse 19: "We have become like those over whom you have never ruled, like those who are not called by your name" (ESV).

The prophet took up the people's cry in his prayer and pleaded with the Lord to reveal Himself anew to Israel as He had done in former times (64:1–3). With eloquent words he reminded the Lord of the rewards promised to those who waited upon Him: "Since ancient times no one has heard, no ear has perceived, no eye has seen any God besides you, who acts on behalf of those who wait for him" (64:4, NIV; see also 30:18; 33:2; 40:31; 49:23). It was this promise that Paul quoted centuries later early in his first letter to the Christians at Corinth (1 Corinthians 2:9–10).

The remainder of the prophet's prayer resembles the penitential laments found in the book of Psalms (see Psalms 6; 32:1–5; 38; 51; 102; 130; 143). He acknowledged that the people of Jerusalem are sinners: "We have all become like one who is unclean, and all our righteous deeds are like a polluted garment. We all fade like a leaf, and our iniquities, like the wind, take us away" (64:6, ESV). Then, too, we can't miss the pathos in his lament over Jerusalem and the Temple: "Our holy and glorious temple, where our ancestors praised you, has been burned with fire, and all that we treasured lies in ruins" (64:10–11, NIV; see Psalm 137:5–6). And in his final appeal the prophet prays, "After all this, LORD, will you hold yourself back? Will you keep silent and punish us beyond measure?" (64:12, NIV).

Prophecies of Judgment and Salvation (65:1–66:24)

God's Love Rejected

The first of these prophecies opens with God sounding like a rejected lover (65:1–7): "I was ready to be sought by those who did not ask for me; I was ready to be found by those who did not seek me. I said, 'Here I am, here I am,' to a nation that was not called by my name" (65:1, ESV).

God's eagerness to show His love to His people and His readiness to be found by them is emphasized in verse 1. It is reminiscent of a game of hide-and-seek in which the hiding player wants to be found and calls out to reveal himself. God invites us to seek Him, while at the same time He makes Himself accessible to us. Perhaps this is what the prophet had in mind when he said, "Seek the LORD while he may be found; call on him while he is near" (55:6, NIV). The Lord's readiness to be found always exceeds our readiness to seek Him.

Unfortunately, though, we are all too often much like the ancient Israelites, who refused to hear the Lord's gracious invitation to seek Him. Although they had only recently been rescued from Babylon, a considerable number of them had already lapsed into their old sinful ways. The prophet pictures God with outstretched arms inviting the people to come, but instead they reject his invitation and go their own way (65:1–2). They were also guilty of participating in acts of pagan worship (65:3), such as sitting in graves, perhaps in order to consult the spirits of the dead (65:4), and they disobeyed the ancient dietary laws by eating "the flesh of pigs" (65:4, NIV; Leviticus 11:7). In spite of their sinful practices, they apparently had the arrogant "holier than thou" notion that they were so special that their pagan neighbors shouldn't even come near them (65:5). This sounds like the Pharisees who opposed Jesus, and especially the one who prayed, "God, I thank you that I am not like other men, extortioners, unjust, adulterers, or *even like this tax collector*" (Luke 18:11, ESV; italics added for emphasis).

With that kind of attitude in the Jerusalem community, not even God would come near them as He compared them to smoke from a foul-smelling fire that never went out (65:5). At the same time, He reminded them that He was well aware of their disobedience, and they would have to suffer the consequences of their sin (65:6–7).

The Sparing of a Righteous Remnant

The prophet next employed a vintage proverb to show them that their only hope for survival was with the righteous few who were still a part of the Jerusalem community (65:8; see 6:13; 10:20–22; 28:5; 37:31–32). The notion that a few righteous persons could save an entire city or nation from destruction was rooted in such stories as that of Abraham's intercession on behalf of Sodom (see Genesis 18:22–33).

The prophet made it clear, however, that in the present situation the righteous people could save only themselves. His idea of individual responsibility closely resembled that of the prophet Ezekiel (see Ezekiel 18:20), as it is made clear that only the righteous people would inherit the Holy Land and only their descendants would live there and enjoy the glorious future of the true servants of the Lord (65:9–16).

New Heavens and a New Earth

The prophet next expanded upon the glorious future awaiting the Lord's faithful servants by announcing the creation of new heavens and a new earth (65:17–25). In the prophecy we have a marvelous picture of that New Jerusalem—that idyllic time when "the wolf and the lamb will feed together" (verse 25, NIV). The description of this new creation is similar in many respects to the Garden of Eden.

What kind of earth does the prophet see after God had recreated it? First of all, it would be an earth where weeping was replaced by rejoicing (65:18–19). Second, it would be a place where premature death was eliminated and everyone would live to a ripe old age (65:20). Third, earth's inhabitants would be able to live to enjoy the fruits of their labor (65:21–23). Fourth, God would grant the requests of His people even before they asked, and their prayers would never fall on deaf ears (65:24). Fifth, all of earth's creatures would live together in peace and harmony, as even the wild beasts would lose their ferocity (65:25; see 11:6–9).

The prophet foresaw a return to the ideal state that existed in the Garden of Eden before Adam and Eve sinned.

This meant that the long-term effects of their sin would be reversed. The Septuagint and the Targum, the two most ancient translations of the Hebrew Bible, made an addition at the end of verse 22 that reads, "For like the days of *the tree of life* shall be the days of my people." Early Jewish interpreters saw in this passage a recurrence of the Garden of Eden motif (see Genesis 2:9; 3:24; Ezekiel 47:1–12; Revelation 22:1–2, 14). The closing statement in verse 25 meant that when the Lord created new heavens and a new earth, no living creature would hurt or destroy another living creature, and this would apply to both human beings and animals. This was God's blueprint for a kinder, gentler earth.

The Requirements of True Worship

Chapter 66 opens with the announcement that the God who has heaven as His throne and earth as His footstool does not dwell in temples made by human hands (66:1; see Acts 7:48–50). Rather, He lives with those who have a humble and contrite spirit and who revere His words (66:2; see 57:15). We are reminded here of the definition of true worship given later by Jesus, "But a time is coming, and even now has arrived, when the true worshippers will worship the Father in spirit and truth; for such people the Father seeks to be His worshippers. God is spirit, and those who worship Him must worship in spirit and truth" (John 4:23–24, NASB).

The people who are most pleasing and acceptable to God are not the rich and famous or those most likely to get their names in *Who's Who.* Rather, they are the humble and contrite, the lowly of spirit who are attentive to God's Word. They are the

Hannahs (see 1 Samuel 1:1–2:11), the Marys (see Luke 1:38, 46–47), and the poor widows whose poverty does not dampen their generous spirits (see Luke 21:1–4). They are the unsung heroes who quietly maintain their loyalty to God even under the most trying circumstances, and those who serve God with no expectation of reward, except the reward of knowing Him better. Perhaps you have been fortunate enough in your Christian pilgrimage to meet people like this. They are the ones Jesus referred to as the salt of the earth and the light of the world. Isaiah might well have called them the friends of God.

Several of the words of the Lord as translated in verse 3 of the New American Standard Bible are in italics; other Bible translations do this as well. Bible translators do this when words are missing from or were illegible or undiscernible in the original text; it is their way of telling the reader that the italicized words were extrapolated and filled in by the translators according to their knowledge and understanding as well as the context of the surrounding text. You will see the italicized words here in the NASB: "*But* the one who slaughters an ox is *like* one who kills a person; the one who sacrifices a lamb is *like* one who breaks a dog's neck; one who offers a grain offering *is like one who offers* pig's blood; one who burns incense is *like* one who blesses an idol. As they have chosen their *own* ways, and their souls delight in their abominations, so I will choose their punishments and bring on them what they dread" (66:3–4). Even in the unlikely event that the translators might have extrapolated incorrectly, the meaning here is clear: the Lord was condemning the combining of legitimate, God-ordained forms of sacrifice and worship with illegitimate forms borrowed from Israel's idol-worshipping pagan neighbors. What most offended the Lord was that the people were mixing acceptable and unacceptable acts in their worship of Him.

The prophet then announced that because the people had chosen their own ways (66:3), God would also choose to delude and confound them (66:4). In other words, they had made their move, but God would now make His. They were free to make their own choice, but it was God who determined the consequences.

A Voice from the Temple

Apparently there was a division in the Jerusalem community whereby certain of the faithful Jews were persecuted by their brethren who "cast" them out (66:5–6). "Cast you out" (ESV) probably means to be cut off from the Temple and the worship that was done there (see Jeremiah 36:5; John 9:22, 34–35). Those who did the casting out were most likely the civil and religious authorities in the community. They supposed that by so doing they were actually serving the Lord, for they said, "Let the Lord be glorified" (ESV).

There have been people in every generation who consider themselves protectors of the status quo who are ready to persecute others "in the name of the Lord" (see John 16:2). The prophet announced, however, that when the day of judgment came, those who had cast their brethren out of the Temple would hear the voice of the Lord pronouncing judgment upon them (66:6). They could silence their own brethren, but they couldn't silence the Lord.

Peace Like a River

The prophet continues now to draw a distinction between the righteous group and the wicked element within Israel (66:7–14). The images employed in this prophecy are those of a mother giving birth to her son and of her feeding and loving care. The picture here is of the future birth of a new nation with Jerusalem as the mother. And even as "mother Jerusalem" cares for and nurtures the infant people, so God will also comfort the righteous like a mother.

Judgment by Fire

Next follows a description in colorful language of the Lord's coming to judge the wicked by fire (66:15–17). Singled out for special condemnation were those who had participated in forbidden cult practices borrowed from pagan religions (66:17). These included such practices as sacrificing "in gardens" (65:3, KJV) and eating forbidden foods (see Leviticus 11:7, 29).

Marching to Zion

The book of Isaiah begins with a description of the desolate condition of Jerusalem resulting from Sennacherib's attack upon the city in 701 BC (see 1:2–9). The final verses in the book present an interesting mirroring of this beginning (66:15–17). Once again the nations are pictured as marching to Zion, but this time they are not coming to attack but to honor her and to participate in the worship of the true God.

The vision is one of worldwide recognition of Israel's God as the only God and of Jerusalem as His place of worship. Those who come to worship will not only see God's glory

(66:18) but will also go out to be witnesses of His glory across the world (66:19). The displaced and scattered people of Jerusalem will return from the ends of the earth by every conceivable means of transportation (66:20). Because of the mass influx of people, the need for worship leaders will be so great that some of the returning exiles will be chosen to serve as priests and Levites. They will help provide for the steady stream of pilgrims coming up to Jerusalem to worship the Lord (66:21–23). The prophet apparently expected these things to take place during his own lifetime.

The Destruction of the Ungodly

The prophet's final words speak of severe judgment on those who reject the Lord (66:24). The gruesome description is terrifying. Jesus quoted from verse 24's imagery in Mark 9:48 (see verses 43–49). The shocking words here and in Mark remind us that hell—the place where the worm does not die and the fire is not quenched (see Revelation 11:9–10; 20:10, 14–15)—is not far from Heaven.

A Final Word

To avoid ending the book of Isaiah on such a somber note, ancient Jewish rabbis gave instructions that when the final chapter was read aloud in the synagogues, verse 23 should be repeated after verse 24. But we need to be reminded that if we reject the Lord, merely rearranging the verses will not provide a happy ending.

The prophet himself vividly contrasts for us the consequences of obedience and disobedience: "You will keep in perfect peace those whose minds are steadfast, because they trust in you" (Isaiah 26:3, NIV); "But the wicked are like the tossing sea, which cannot rest, whose waves cast up mire and mud. 'There is no peace,' says my God, 'for the wicked'" (57:20–21, NIV).

Despite its complex nature, the book of Isaiah has a very practical application to the believers and churches of today. One of its fundamental messages is that unity, wholeness, peace, wellness, and spiritual understanding are the results of a life lived in obedience to the will and plan of God. This is not some esoteric and difficult goal to attain. Rather it comes through a daily application of Jesus's teachings to the nitty-gritty of our twenty-four-hour days. To reject God is to invite the consequences of a selfish and sinful life. To accept God as the center of our life is to find peace even in our hard times.

Father, may You always be the center of my life.
Help me to always be centered on You. Amen.

The least of you will become a thousand, the smallest a mighty nation. I am the Lord; in its time I will do this swiftly.

—Isaiah 60:22 (NIV)

For an animal so small, they make a powerful noise. Not only are peepers loud, but their chorus is almost always a welcome one. Their song announces the coming of spring.

The snow had barely melted late last March when my husband, Mike, and I went out to walk the dogs. It was one of those nights when the air smelled green and wet, and I had a bounce in my step, knowing that spring was just around the corner. Then I heard it—the high-pitched chorus of PEEP PEEP PEEP. Among the tiny frogs, the males make the loud noise to attract mates. There must have been dozens of them peeping. Together, they sounded like the jingle of sleigh bells.

"Oh, don't you just love peepers?" I said.

"We used to hear them every spring when my family went to the lake," Mike answered.

Although they're easy to miss, I remember finding one and picking it up when I was a child. The little peeper was brown, less than an inch long, with sticky toe pads, and it surely weighed less than an ounce. It had a dark cross pattern on its back. Their scientific name is *Pseudacris crucifer*, the latter word meaning "cross-bearing" or "cross-bearer."

At the time I didn't think anything spiritual of it, but now I do. All God's creatures have the potential to teach me something spiritual. Peepers are barely noticeable during the day. But when they sing, one can't miss them. There are times when I feel insignificant and powerless. When I do, I remember the peepers. God made them small but mighty.

—Peggy Frezon

Notes

Notes

Notes

Acknowledgments

Every attempt has been made to credit the sources of copyrighted material used in this book. If any such acknowledgment has been inadvertently omitted or miscredited, receipt of such information would be appreciated.

Scripture quotations marked (AMP) are taken from the *Amplified Bible*.

Scripture quotations marked (ESV) are taken from *The Holy Bible, English Standard Version*.

Scripture quotations marked (KJV) are taken from the *King James Version of the Bible*.

Scripture quotations marked (NASB) are taken from the *New American Standard Bible®*.

Scripture quotations marked (NIV) are taken from *The Holy Bible, New International Version®, NIV®*.

A Note from the Editors

We hope you enjoyed *Living with Purpose Bible Study: Isaiah* published by Guideposts. For over 75 years, Guideposts, a nonprofit organization, has been driven by a vision of a world filled with hope. We aspire to be the voice of a trusted friend, a friend who makes you feel more hopeful and connected.

By making a purchase from Guideposts, you join our community in touching millions of lives, inspiring them to believe that all things are possible through faith, hope, and prayer. Your continued support allows us to provide uplifting resources to those in need. Whether through our communities, websites, apps, or publications, we inspire our audiences, bring them together, and comfort, uplift, entertain, and guide them. Visit us at guideposts.org to learn more.

We would love to hear from you. Write us at Guideposts, P.O. Box 5815, Harlan, Iowa 51593 or call us at (800) 932-2145. Did you love *Living with Purpose Bible Study: Isaiah*? Leave a review for this product on guideposts.org/shop. Your feedback helps others in our community find relevant products.

Printed in the United States
by Baker & Taylor Publisher Services